CHRISTMAS GIFTS
for you to make

ALSO BY SUSAN PURDY

CHRISTMAS DECORATIONS FOR YOU TO MAKE
BOOKS FOR YOU TO MAKE
COSTUMES FOR YOU TO MAKE
FESTIVALS FOR YOU TO CELEBRATE
JEWISH HOLIDAYS
HOLIDAY CARDS FOR YOU TO MAKE
IF YOU HAVE A YELLOW LION

for muffin

CHRISTMAS GIFTS
for you to make

by
Susan Purdy

J. B. LIPPINCOTT COMPANY / PHILADELPHIA AND NEW YORK

U.S. Library of Congress Cataloging in Publication Data

Purdy, Susan Gold, birth date
    Christmas gifts for you to make.

    SUMMARY: Directions for making a wide variety of useful and decorative gifts suitable
for any occasion.
    1. Handicraft—Juvenile literature. [1. Handicraft. 2. Gifts] I. Title.
TT160.P87   745.59′41   76-10160
ISBN-0-397-31695-X   ISBN-0-397-31696-8 (pbk.)

for my helpers
Tracy & Julie
and Muffin

CONTENTS

GIFT IDEA INDEX

Gifts for Children: Glove Finger Puppets, Pompom Playmates, Paddle Wheel Boat, Grow Tape, Mix-Match Book, Tic-Tac-Toe Wall Hanging, Wood Dolls, Bath Puppet, Learning Pillow

Gifts for Pets: Pets' Christmas Stockings, Catnip Mouse, Pet's Munchies Box

Gifts for Gardeners: Patchwork Flowerpots, Gardening Gloves, Dried Flower Note Cards, Macramé Plant Hanger, Yarn-Covered Flowerpot, Bean Sprouter, Patchwork Apron

Gifts for Game Players: Tic-Tac-Toe Wall Hanging, Domino Scoreboard

Gifts for Desk or Office: Dried Flower Note Cards, Decorative Note Pad, Desk Organizer, Yarn-Covered Box, Lap Desk, String Dispenser Box

Gifts for Home or Table: Thumbtack Mosaic Trivet, Bean Sprouter, Felt Rosebuds, Hair Ribbon or Necktie Rack, Fancy Pin Cushion, Yarn-Covered Gifts, String Dispenser Box, Appliquéd Gifts, Log Carrier, Patchwork Pillow

Gifts to Wear: Dough Designs (jewelry), Gardening Gloves, Paper Beads, Patchwork Aprons

Gifts for Everyone: Dough Designs, Mix-Match Book, Sheepskin Shoe Buffer, Wood Candlesticks and Dolls

ABOUT THIS BOOK

Anyone can go into a store and buy a gift, but only a very special person will devote the time, thought, and effort necessary to *make* a gift. You are that special person, and you can be sure the gifts you make will be treasured and saved, because "made by hand" means made with love.

Some of the gifts in this book are quick and easy to make. Others are more complex and take more time. Be sure to read all the directions through to the end before beginning a project, so you know what materials are needed as well as approximately how long it will take. Start planning and making your gifts well before the holidays so they will be ready in time for Christmas.

All the materials and equipment used in the projects are listed on pages 10 and 11. Directions for basic stitches and hems are on pages 13 and 14. To help select appropriate gifts for the people and pets on your list, see the index on page 8. Gift wrapping and mailing ideas are on page 94.

We hope gift-making, with the help of this book, will become a habitual and happy part of your holiday season.

9

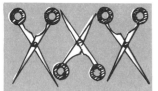 **MATERIALS**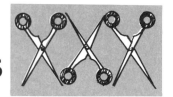

Here is a list of all the materials and equipment used in this book. Each project will require the use of only a few of the things at a time. Materials can be found in your own home, local stationery store, five-and-ten-cent store, art supply or craft shop, fabric or remnant shop, or hardware store. If you have trouble finding the specified material, try substituting something different, or look in the Yellow Pages of the telephone book.

ART and STATIONERY SUPPLIES (found in art supply, hobby, and craft shops; many items can also be found in hardware or stationery stores)

tempera paint, acrylic paint; découpage varnish (optional); crayons, felt-tip pens (waterproof oil-base and washable water-base); pencils, ball point pen or fountain pen and ink; blackboard chalk; *paper:* construction paper, sketch paper, gift wrap, self-adhesive paper, wallpaper (remnants or old sample books are sometimes given away by wallpaper shops), tracing paper; X-Acto knife with any straight-edged blade, or utility knife; scissors; paint brushes; rubber cement, white glue (such as Elmer's or Sobo, which dries clear); *tape:* masking tape, cellophane tape, "write-on" cellophane tape, waterproof colored adhesive tape (such as Mystik tape), florists' tape (found in craft or flower shops); ruler; stapler (one that can be opened out flat); paper clips, thumbtacks, rubber bands; *Styrofoam:* ball (about 5″ diameter), sheet foam about ½″ to 1″ thick, or pressed foam—roughly ⅛″ thick—used as supermarket meat trays, or molded packing material; sheepskin (piece with fur on one side and leather on other side; found in craft and hobby shops, or at furriers', who sometimes sell or give away small scraps); earring and pin backs; modeling clay; macramé cord, cotton string; leather thongs or leather boot laces; candles and candle holders (available in candle or craft shops or from suppliers of candle-making equipment); *wire:* #2 or #32 or #22 spool wire, flexible yet strong stem wire such as #15 (sold in craft shops for making paper flowers); blackboard with wooden edging (roughly 9½″ x 13″); solid-color note cards and matching envelopes; note pad (about 3½″ x 6″)

HARDWARE and CARPENTRY SUPPLIES (found in lumberyards, building supply and hardware stores)

tools: hammer, coping saw or jigsaw (optional), wire cutters (optional), pliers, tinsnips; yardstick; sandpaper; nails, brass brads or carpet tacks, screws; C-shaped wooden brackets for holding up curtain rods; *wood:* unfinished turned-wood spindles, fence post tops and flat caps, shelf spacers, drapery pole finials, scraps of boards (pine or fir), ¼″ to ½″

plywood (optional), dowels (¼" to ½" and 1" to 1½" diameter) or wooden curtain rods or sawed-off broom handles; wood stain, enamel paint, varnish, turpentine or paint thinner (for washing brushes), clear shellac, denatured alcohol shellac solvent (for washing brushes); self-adhesive picture hanger; sheet cork (optional); rope or sisal twine or jute (for macramé hanger), cotton string; nylon fishing line (optional), gardening gloves, flowerpots

SEWING SUPPLIES (found in fabric stores, department stores, five-and-ten-cent stores)
tape measure; pinking shears (optional); sewing needles, darning needle, embroidery needle, knitting needle (optional); thimble; sewing machine (optional); *thread:* heavy-duty, as well as #50 or #60 sewing thread, embroidery thread, elastic thread (optional); iron, ironing board; yarn (wool or acrylic); straight pins, safety pins; tailor's chalk or blackboard chalk; *fabric:* terry toweling or terry cloth, felt, cotton, cheesecloth, permanent press blends, denim or duck, cotton velvet, scraps of trimming material such as lace, fringe, etc.; Velcro tape (double-layered self-gripping fastener tape) or snap fasteners, buttons, zipper; *ribbon:* grosgrain, satin or other fabric ribbon ½" to ¾" wide, velvet cord, binding braid (optional); *pillow stuffing:* cotton batting, quilt lining, foam rubber, kapok, surgical cotton, or clean rags; beads, sequins; café curtain rings

HOUSEHOLD and KITCHEN SUPPLIES and HOME DISCARDS
gloves (solid-color cotton or other cloth; old gloves can be used), socks (for Christmas stockings use very large size or knee socks, made of wool or acrylic); old towels, dish towel; cheesecloth; hand mirror (small plastic-framed pocket mirror, sold in five-and-ten); candles; vase (long-stemmed goblet shape, any material); flowerpots; spring-type clothespins; corks; dominoes or other game parts; clear nail polish, emery board or nail file, tweezers; flowers, leaves, and grasses to press dry; plastic bags; flexible shirt cardboard; egg cartons; plastic drinking straws, paper cup; paper doilies; *boxes:* plastic, wood, cardboard (boxes with and without lids), as well as metal containers; cardboard oatmeal cartons; *kitchen utensils:* mixing bowls, saucepan, measuring cups and spoons, rolling pin, wooden spoon, wire rack, dull knife, skewer, cookie sheet, strainer, spatula, fork, garlic press; glass jar (quart size); can opener, grater, or other textured tools (for pressing designs into dough); baking oven and stove top; *foods:* dry beans and seeds for sprouting (mung, alfalfa, wheat, etc.), cornstarch, baking soda, salt, all-purpose flour, vegetable food coloring, catnip (found in grocery or pet shop or health food store)

BEFORE YOU BEGIN . . .

First, read through all project directions from beginning to end. Assemble all equipment and materials before starting.

For messy projects, protect work surface with old newspapers and protect your clothes with an apron.

Acrylic paint can be cleaned up with water. When using shellac, wash your brushes out in denatured alcohol solvent; when using enamel paint, wood stain, or varnish, wash your brushes in turpentine or paint thinner.

X-Acto knives and utility knives are sharp; you should have either the help or the permission of an adult when using them.

Ask for the help or permission of an adult when using the stove or oven.

Throughout the book, the symbol " has been used for *inches* and ' for *feet*.

METRIC EQUIVALENTS

To convert the measurements in this book into the metric system, use the following table. The measurements given are rounded off to the nearest useful number.

Units Given:	Multiplied by:	Equals:
Inches	2.5	Centimeters
Feet	30	Centimeters
Yards	0.9	Meters
Pounds	454	Grams
Pounds	0.45	Kilograms
Cups	240	Milliliters
Cups	0.24	Liters
Quarts	0.95	Liters

BASIC STITCHES AND HEMS

These drawings show right-handed sewing. If you are left-handed, sew from left to right if that feels more comfortable.

RUNNING STITCH

This is the easiest stitch for general sewing or hemming. Thread needle, knot one end of thread, and stitch as shown. For a hem, make large (1″) stitches on side facing you (a) and small (¼″) stitches through to front. For general sewing, you can make front and back stitches the same size (b).

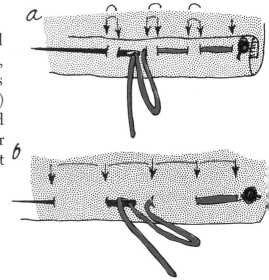

OVERCASTING OR WHIPSTITCH

This stitch is often used to bind cut fabric edges to keep them from unraveling (a). It is also used to join two pieces of fabric placed side by side (b). Take your first stitch from the back side of the fabric; this will keep the knot out of sight. Sew around edges of piece or along edges to be joined, placing stitches close together so they are almost touching.

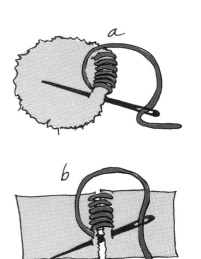

HEMSTITCH

To make a plain hem, turn under and pin the edge of your fabric, as shown. To sew, use running stitch (above), or use this stitch, which is a very common hemstitch. Stitches are placed along edge of hem and slant to one side. Needle goes through a very tiny bit of fabric on the front side (bottom layer), then comes back up and goes through edge of hem as shown.

ROLLED HEM

To make a rolled hem, place fabric *wrong side up* on table. Make first fold (a) by bending the edge over about 1"—or whatever width is specified in directions.

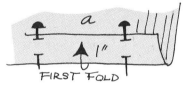

Make second fold (b) by rolling the first under about 1"—or whatever width is specified. Pin hem as shown.

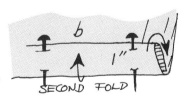

Sew hem using running stitch or hemstitch, or sew by machine.

PUPPET STAGE

GLOVE FINGER PUPPETS

A few bits of felt, paint, and a pen line or two can transform a glove into a gay handful of finger puppets. This is an absorbing project for a rainy day and makes a gift any child will enjoy.

Materials: One or two cloth gloves, sketch paper, pencil, acrylic paint and brush or thin-pointed felt-tip pens or ball-point pen or fountain pen and ink, needle and thread, embroidery thread, scrap material and trimmings (bits of colored felt or other fabric, lace, ribbon, yarn, buttons, beads), white glue, straight pins or paper clips or spring-type clothespins, scissors

1. Set glove flat, *palm side up,* on sketch paper. Draw around it to make an outline, as shown.

   Design puppets on paper first; faces will be on palm side of fingertips, and bodies—if you want to make them—along length of fingers. Puppets can have any personality you like. For example, they can be members of a family, different characters from a book, animals, or imaginary creatures.

WHOLE HAND DESIGNED ON PAPER FIRST

2. Use paints or pens or needle and thread to make puppets' faces. Sew on yarn or embroidery thread hair. Paint, sew, or glue on fabric or felt hats, ears, and clothes. Trim with buttons, lace, or beads. Use clothespins or paper clips or pins to hold freshly glued trimmings in place on glove until dry.

3. The glove, or gloves, can be decorated and left whole as shown above, or you can make separate finger puppets by cutting the fingers off the glove. Sew overcast stitch (page 13) around cut bottom edges to keep them from unraveling.

CUT OFF FINGERS OF GLOVE

15

POMPOM PLAYMATES

Everyone will love these funny wool toys. Give one pompom or several, each a different creature. Or make five or six and hang them on a mobile.

Materials: Cardboard, ruler, scissors, wool or acrylic yarn (the bulkier the better), thin yarn or button thread, sketch paper, pencil, felt scraps, needle and thread or white glue, straight pins or paper clips

1. To make a 3″ diameter pompom, cut cardboard 3″ x 5″. Wrap 4 or 5 yards of bulky yarn (or more if yarn is thin) around the long sides of the cardboard as shown.

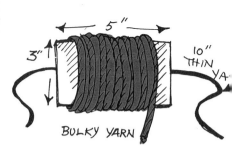

BULKY YARN

2. Cut a 10″ length of thin yarn or button thread and set it flat on the table. Place yarn-wrapped card over it as shown.

3. Slide scissors blade along top edge of cardboard as shown and cut through all the loops of yarn. Repeat on bottom edge. Slip out the card.

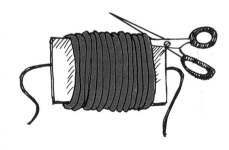

4. Tie the ends of the thin yarn together over the centers of the bulky yarn. Knot thin yarn. If making a hanging toy, leave the ends of this thin yarn long, or tie on an extra piece of yarn for a hanger. Fluff out the yarn around the central knot, making a rounded ball. Use scissors to trim uneven ends.

5. Design your creatures by sketching them first on scrap paper. Keep all shapes simple and bold. To make eyes, cut two ½″ circles of white or light blue felt. On top of these circles, glue pupils made from ¼″ circles or ovals of a darker blue. A beak or snout can be cut from a triangular piece of felt about 2″ x 1½″; a bird's tail and wings can be made from pieces about 2″ x 2″. Use paper clips or straight pins to hold the pieces of felt in place on the wool pom-pom while the glue is drying; when glue is dry, remove all paper clips or pins.

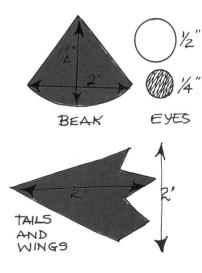

BEAK   EYES

TAILS AND WINGS

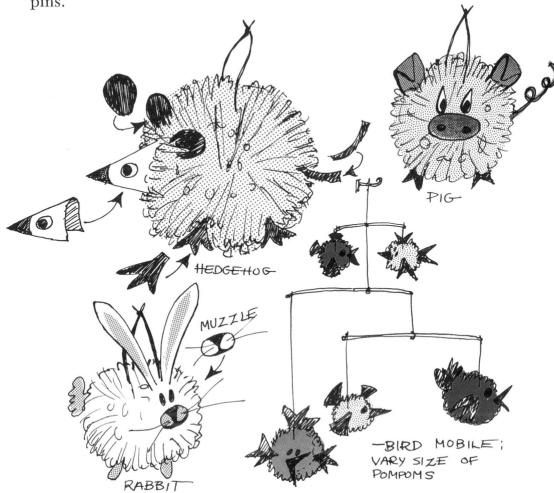

HEDGEHOG

PIG

MUZZLE

RABBIT

BIRD MOBILE; VARY SIZE OF POMPOMS

DOUGH DESIGNS

Both the following recipes use common kitchen ingredients, but the dough is *not* meant to be eaten. It is meant to be used like clay. Shape it into any form you like, from jewelry to dolls to Christmas tree ornaments. Designs made with either dough will last indefinitely when coated with shellac or varnish to keep out moisture. Shapes made of cornstarch dough can be dried in the air; baker's clay shapes must be dried in the oven.

Materials: Ingredients for cornstarch dough or baker's clay (see below); saucepan, mixing bowl, measuring cup, large spoon (preferably wooden), wax paper or plate, clean cloth or dish towel, airtight container or plastic bag, rolling pin, cookie sheet, toothpicks, wire rack, cookie cutter or jar or glass, small kitchen knife, cardboard pattern (optional), spatula, skewer, knitting needle, scissors, tools and objects for texturing and trimming (fork, cheese grater, bottle caps; chips of broken glass or mirror, beads, sequins, etc.), emery board or nail file or fine sandpaper, tempera or acrylic paint and brushes, clear shellac or varnish or nail polish, wire or button thread or thin ribbon (for hanging ornaments), white glue and pin backs (for jewelry)

CORNSTARCH DOUGH

Ingredients: 1 cup cornstarch
2 cups baking soda
1¼ cups cold water
food coloring (optional)

NOTE: BAKER'S CLAY ON PG. 22

1. Place cornstarch and baking soda in saucepan and mix well. Then stir in cold water. If you want to color entire batch of dough, add a few drops of food coloring along with water.

2. **With help or permission of an adult,** place saucepan on stove over medium heat and stir continually with wooden spoon until mixture is as thick as mashed potatoes. Remove pan from heat and turn dough out onto a piece of wax paper or a plate. Cover with a damp (*not* dripping wet) cloth or dish towel and let it cool for about 30 minutes.

18

3. Cover work area with wax paper. When dough is cool, set it in one big lump on wax paper and knead until smooth by folding the lump over on itself and pushing down on it with the palm of your hand. Repeat, kneading for about 2 minutes. Store dough in airtight container or plastic bag and remove pieces as needed. Dough will dry out if left in the air.

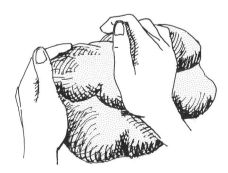

4. Shape designs following Basic Shaping Directions below.

Cornstarch dough designs will usually dry overnight, but very thick pieces can take longer. To shorten drying time, set designs on a wire rack so air can circulate on all sides of dough. If you are in a rush, you can bake dough until hard on a cookie sheet in a warm (180° to 200°) oven. Test hardness every 15 minutes or so. **Use oven only with help or permission of an adult.**

Designs will have a smooth, easily worked surface. Rough edges can be smoothed by scraping with an emery board or nail file. To polish a surface, rub with fine sandpaper or the fine surface of an emery board.

Complete designs following Basic Finishing Directions.

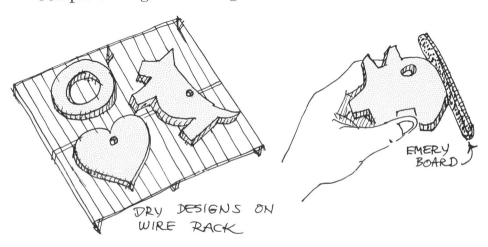

DRY DESIGNS ON WIRE RACK

EMERY BOARD

BASIC SHAPING DIRECTIONS

After preparing dough, there are many different ways to model it. For example, you can roll the dough with a rolling pin on or between sheets of wax paper until it is about ⅛″ to ¼″ thick. Then cut shapes as you would cut cookies, using a jar or glass top or cookie cutter to press shapes into the dough. If the cutter sticks, dip it in cornstarch or flour before pressing it into the dough. Or use the point of a small knife to cut any shape you like. You can trace around your own cardboard pattern on the dough with the point of a knife. You can also trace lightly around your own outstretched hand with the point of a toothpick, then take away the hand and cut through the marked outlines on the dough. Cornstarch dough can be either left to dry on the wax paper or lifted onto a wire rack with a floured spatula. Baker's clay shapes should be left on the wax paper, which is placed directly on the cookie sheet for baking.

You can also roll and model dough into three-dimensional forms as you would clay. To color individual pieces of dough, knead in drops of food coloring. To stick one piece of dough to another, first put a drop of water on the place where the pieces will join. To make fingers, toes, hair, etc., cut strips in dough with scissors. To make beads, roll round or oval balls of dough. Poke hole in each ball with toothpick or thin knitting needle dipped in cornstarch or flour. Remove needle and dry dough.

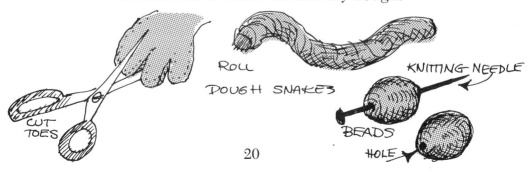

Textures and patterns can be pressed into the dough with nearly any object: for example, the tines of a fork make stripes, the side of a cheese grater makes a crisscross pattern or fish scales, a can opener makes sharp points. Press a lump of dough through a garlic press to make hair for a figure or shaggy coat for a dog. Model a face with a toothpick. Press chips of colored glass or broken bits of mirror or other scrap materials into designs for sparkle—especially for tree ornaments.

Use a toothpick or skewer to poke the hanging hole for an ornament in top of design before it hardens or is baked.

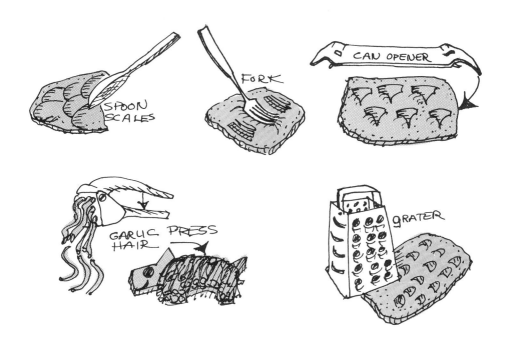

BASIC FINISHING DIRECTIONS

After completing designs, paint them (unless previously colored with food coloring) with tempera or acrylic paints and let them dry well. Then paint clear shellac or varnish or nail polish over the front of each piece and let it dry well; turn piece over and coat the back and sides. This will keep shapes hard. Finally, glue pin backs onto dough shapes; string beads onto lengths of button thread; and tie wire, thread, or ribbon loops in hanging ornaments.

21

BAKER'S CLAY

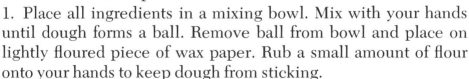

Ingredients: 4 cups all-purpose flour
1 cup salt
1½ cups water

1. Place all ingredients in a mixing bowl. Mix with your hands until dough forms a ball. Remove ball from bowl and place on lightly floured piece of wax paper. Rub a small amount of flour onto your hands to keep dough from sticking.

2. Knead dough until it is smooth and holds together well. To do this, fold dough over on itself and push down on it with the palms of your hands. Repeat, kneading for about 2 minutes. If dough feels dry and crumbly, add a few drops of water as you knead. Place dough in airtight container or plastic bag and remove pieces as needed. Dough will dry out if left in the air.

3. To roll out baker's clay, cut two pieces of wax paper the same size as your cookie sheet. Lightly flour one piece and place dough on it. Lightly flour dough and cover it with second paper. Roll until dough is about ¼″ thick. If top paper wrinkles, peel it off and reposition it, smoothing it flat. Finally, remove top paper and cut out designs, following Basic Shaping Directions. Peel away extra dough from around shapes.

4. Baker's clay is baked in the oven. **This should be done only with the help or permission of an adult.**

Slide the wax paper holding the designs onto a cookie sheet. Paper will not burn if directions are followed. Bake about 45 minutes in a preheated 325° oven until dough is slightly golden. A toothpick stuck into the thickest part of the dough should come out clean. Cool design on cookie sheet or wire rack before painting. To finish, see Basic Finishing Directions.

This is a toy any child can make and every child will enjoy. Constructed from discarded packaging material (or wood scraps) and a rubber band, the paddle wheel boat will quickly become a bathtub or pond favorite. If you are making a gift for someone with brothers and sisters, make two boats so they can have boat races.

Materials for either boat: Pencil or felt-tip pen, ruler, sketch paper, scissors, masking tape, white glue, rubber band (average size, about 2½" to 3" unstretched), colored plastic Mystik tape. *For wood boat:* Scraps of ½" and ¼" plywood, jigsaw or coping saw, two ½"-long brass brads or tacks, dowel or wood pencil, enamel paint or stain or shellac and brush. *For foam boat:* Pressed foam supermarket meat trays (usually about ⅛" thick) or 1" or ½"-thick sheet Styrofoam (sold in five-and-ten and craft supply stores) or molded Styrofoam packing material (often found in boxes containing new appliances, cameras, etc.), utility or X-Acto knife, plastic drinking straw, waterproof felt-tip pens or crayons

This boat can be made from any material that will float. It is basically a U-shaped design with a paddle wheel connected to the legs of the U by a rubber band. You wind up the rubber band by turning the paddle wheel. When it is released in the water, the rubber band unwinds, turning the wheel, which pushes the boat.

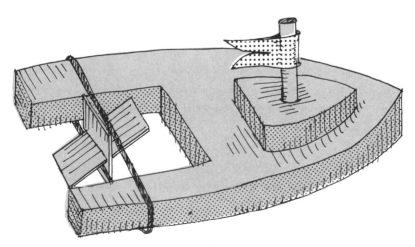

You can make your boat any size and design you like, as long as you understand the following basic ideas. The paddle wheel should be small enough to fit between the legs of the U, with some space on each side of it for winding up the rubber band. When wound, the rubber band pulls tightly against the sides of the boat (the legs of the U). A wooden boat is strong enough to withstand the strain, but the sides of a foam boat might collapse if unsupported. For added strength, our foam boats are designed with a closed back edge and a rectangular hole in which the paddle wheel sits.

1. The boats in our examples are 3″ x 6″. To make basic shape, cut a 3″ x 6″ rectangle of pressed foam, Styrofoam, or ½″ plywood. Use scissors or knife to cut foam (a); use saw to cut plywood. **Be sure you have help or permission of an adult when using knife or jigsaw.**

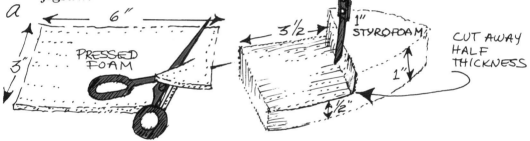

2. Cut front end of boat into any curved shape you like. If using 1″ Styrofoam, leave the front of the boat the full thickness, but cut away half the thickness from the top around the three back sides.

3. To make paddle wheel hole in rear of boat, cut a paper pattern 2½″ square. On a foam boat, position pattern about 3″ back from prow as shown (a), leaving ½″ margins around the three back sides. On a wood boat, position pattern with one edge flat against back end of boat as shown (b), leaving ½″ margins on two sides. Use two small bits of tape to hold pattern down while you draw around it. Cut around drawn shape.

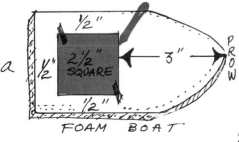

24

4. To add a raised deck on front of boat, cut a foam or wood triangle and glue it to top of boat.

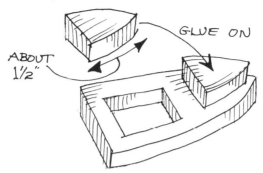

5. To make paddle wheel, cut two 1″ x 2″ pieces of ¼″ plywood (for wood boat) or pressed foam (for pressed foam or Styrofoam boat). In the middle of one long side of each piece (1″ from end), cut a notch ½″ deep and as wide as your material is thick—⅛″ for pressed foam, ¼″ for plywood (a).

Fit notched edges together (b) until sides are even and pieces form a cross (c). If necessary, add a few drops of glue to secure sides. Let glue dry.

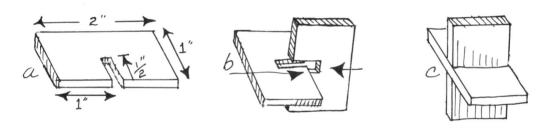

6. Paddle wheel is fastened to the boat with a rubber band. To hold this rubber band in place on a foam boat, cut a small notch in the middle of each side, 1½″ from back end (a). On a wood boat, hammer a brad or tack partway into the top surface of each side, 1″ in from back end (b).

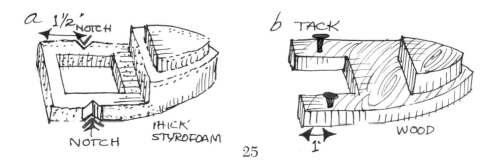

7. To make flagpole for a foam boat, cut a 2″ or 3″ length of plastic drinking straw. For a wood flagpole, cut a dowel or pencil the same length.

8. Sand any rough edges on wood boat. Decorate boat and flagpole with enamel paint or stain or shellac (just to seal the wood). Decorate pressed foam boat with waterproof felt-tip pens or crayons; color Styrofoam boat with waterproof felt-tip pens.

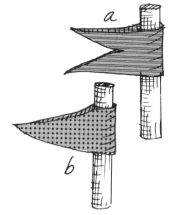

9. To make flag, cut a 3″ length of plastic tape. Center tape around one end of flagpole and press sticky sides of tape together. Cut ends of tape into points as shown (a or b). For foam boat, you can push pole down into the foam before adding a drop of glue to hold it firmly in place. Glue flagpole to front of wood boat.

10. To complete, stretch a rubber band around notched sides of foam boat (a) or between brads or tacks of wooden boat (b). Fit paddle wheel between legs of rubber band as shown (c and d). To wind up wheel push it around and around toward the back end of the boat (arrows, d) until rubber band is twisted taut. The more twists, the farther the boat will travel. Set boat in water and release paddle wheel; as rubber band unwinds, paddle wheel turns, pushing the boat.

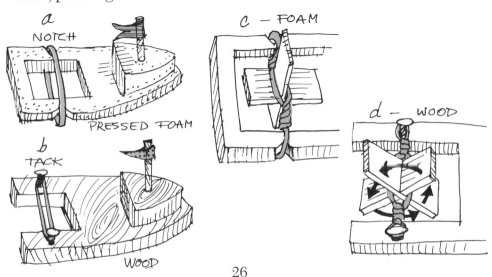

 # GROW TAPE

A grow tape makes a good gift for a new baby or a young child. The tape is attached to a wall, and the child stands beside it to measure and mark his or her height and the date. The tape is a decorative record of growth and can be used until the child is 5 feet tall.

Materials: One 60"-long measuring tape (preferably new, made of brightly colored cloth or plastic), white glue, pencil. *For wood tape:* A strip of wood 60" (5') long by 5" wide, hand saw, sandpaper, acrylic or enamel paint and brush. *For felt or fabric tape:* A strip of felt or other fabric 60" (5') long by 5" wide, scissors, needle and thread, pinking shears (optional), fabric or felt scraps, iron

1. To make a wooden grow tape, measure a board 60" long by 5" wide. **Ask an adult to help you cut board with saw.** Use sandpaper to smooth all rough edges. Paint the wood a solid color all over.

2. To make a felt or fabric tape, cut your material 60" x 5". If material is not long enough, cut shorter strips and sew them together. Iron seams flat on back side. To keep fabric from unraveling at the edges, cut with pinking shears, or fold under and sew a ½" hem around all sides. Iron flat. Cut felt with regular scissors and do not hem.

3. Set your wood or fabric or felt flat on the floor, *right side up.* Glue the tape measure onto the left edge as shown, with the 60" mark at the top. Leave a plain 2" space to the right of the tape measure where the child can write in height and date with a felt-tip pen. Decorate the rest of the area with painted designs or cutout and glued-on felt or fabric shapes.

MIX-MATCH BOOK

This is an inexpensive and easy gift to make, and the lucky person who receives it will enjoy creating funny-looking characters by mix-matching the pages.

Materials: Drawing or construction paper (four or more pieces at least 8½" x 11"), stapler, 1" or 1½" wide colored cloth tape or plastic Mystik tape, ruler, pencil, scissors, crayons or felt-tip pens or old magazines and rubber cement

1. Gather all the pages together and fold them in half crosswise (a). Press along fold. To hold pages together, place six staples parallel to the fold and about ½" inside it as shown (b). To make spine strong, fold a length of tape in half over it (c).

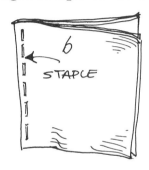

2. To divide the book into three equal horizontal sections, either use a ruler or take a piece of scrap paper the same height as your book and fold it into thirds. Then mark off the width of the folded paper against both the sides of the book. Draw lines connecting marks, but do not draw across spine tape (a). Following lines, cut through all the pages of the book—up to, but not across, spine (b). The book is now divided into three sections, held together only at the spine. We will call the top section 1, the middle 2, and the bottom 3.

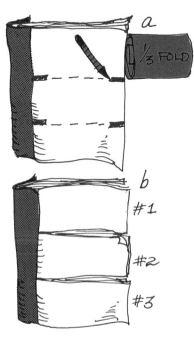

3. On the first (outside) page, make book's cover by drawing a picture of a figure with its head and neck in section 1, its body and arms in section 2, and its legs in section 3. Instead of drawing, you can cut out pictures from magazines and glue them down.

4. Lift up and fold over section 1 of the first page. On the blank section 1 facing you, draw or glue down the head of another figure, lining it up so it fits onto the body below it (a). Then lift up section 2 of the first page and draw or glue down the body of your new figure, lining it up with its own head in section 1 and with the feet in section 3 (b). Finally, lift up section 3 of the first page and add the feet of your new figure so that they fit together with the rest of the body (c).

5. To complete the book, repeat step 4 with each page, adding the head, body, and legs of different figures one section at a time, each piece lined up with the next. You can make funny-looking characters by mix-matching the pages to combine a head from one figure, a body from another, and legs from a third.

TIC-TAC-TOE WALL HANGING

Everyone who likes to play tic-tac-toe will enjoy the game more than ever with this gift, a unique decorative wall hanging made of felt and trimmed with markers that attach with Velcro self-gripping tape or snaps. It can be used to play the game over and over or to decorate the wall of a bedroom or gameroom.

Materials: Felt (two contrasting pieces at least 18″ square, plus scraps of other bright colors), tape measure or ruler, chalk, scissors, straight pins, white glue (optional), needle and thread, sewing machine (optional), 10″ of Velcro (nylon self-gripping fastener) tape or 10 snaps (size 3 or larger), 20″ of wood dowel ¼″ to ½″ in diameter, 36″ of string or colored macramé cord

1. To make background panel, cut an 18″ square of felt. Set panel flat on table. Measure and draw dotted chalk lines 2″ in from top and bottom edges.

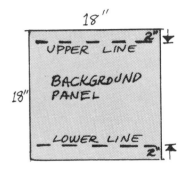

2. To make borders, select a color of felt that contrasts well with background panel (green borders on red, for example). Cut two 2″ x 18″ strips of this color to make side borders. From the same color, also cut out one strip 6″ x 18″ for the top border, and one strip 4″ x 18″ for the bottom border. Cut four strips, each 1″ by 18″, to divide the squares.

3. To decorate bottom border, set 4″ by 18″ strip flat on table and draw a dotted chalk line dividing the strip in half lengthwise (2″ from each long edge, as shown). Below this line, cut seven or eight freehand points. Or, if you prefer, draw around the corner of a box or book to make points, or draw around the rim of a glass or jar to make scallops.

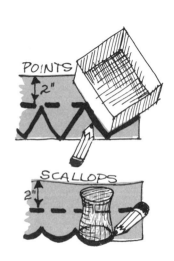

30

4. Place a 2″-wide border strip along each side of background panel. Fold 6″-wide strip in half over top edge of panel, lining up long sides of strip with upper dotted line. Also place 4″-wide pointed or scalloped strip along bottom edge of panel, lining up long smooth side of strip with lower dotted line.

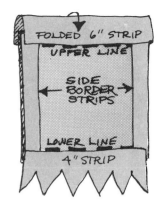

5. Area inside borders should now measure about 14″ x 14″. Divide this space into nine equal squares using the 1″-wide strips. To do this, first position the two horizontal strips 4″ apart; then, crossing over them, place the two vertical strips 4″ apart.

Hide ends of dividing strips by tucking them under the wide borders. Pin all strips and borders in place. Keep outside edges of side borders lined up with background panel; keep top and bottom borders lined up along panel's dotted chalk lines. There should be a 1″-deep pocket beneath the fold of the top border to hold the hanging rod.

6. Glue or sew down all strips and borders. If sewing, stitch along *all* edges by hand using a running stitch (page 13) or on a sewing machine. Cut off all hanging threads on front and back of panel.

7. To make markers, use two different colors of felt that contrast well with background panel. We used gold and bright blue. Out of one color, cut five circles about 2″ to 2½″ across. Out of the second color, cut five triangles or other shapes such as hearts, flowers, crosses, or diamonds roughly 2″ to 2½″ across. Cut unusual shapes freehand or draw around a paper pattern.

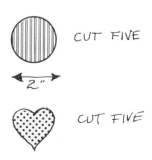

8. If you are using Velcro, you will see that it consists of two pieces of tape which grip when pressed together. One piece is covered with fuzzy loops, the other with hooks. Press both 10″ pieces together. Cutting through both layers at once, make ten segments, each 1″ long. Peel each segment apart and sew a looped half in the center of each square on the background panel as shown. Sew the last looped segment onto the center of the *wrong* side of the panel. Sew the hooked half of each Velcro segment in the center of the back of each marker. You can either sew around all four edges of the Velcro or just along its smooth borders.

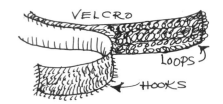

SEW LAST PIECE ON BACK SIDE OF PANEL

If you are using snaps, you will see that each is made up of two separate halves. In the middle of each square on the background panel, sew the half that has the knob sticking up. Sew the last of these pieces onto the center of the *wrong* side of the panel. Sew the other half of each snap in the center of the back of each marker.

HOOKED HALF OF TAPE SEWN TO MARKER'S BACK SIDE

KNOB

SNAP

There are nine squares on the tic-tac-toe panel and ten markers. When not playing the game, leave nine of the markers in place on the front of the panel and store the extra (tenth) marker on the tape or snap you have sewn to the panel's wrong side.

9. To make hanging rod, push dowel through pocket in top border. Tie one end of 36″ string to each end of dowel and hang string on hook or nail.

DOMINO SCOREBOARD

Trim a small blackboard with a frame of dominoes—or other discarded game parts—to create a unique playroom or gameroom gift.

Materials: Blackboard with wooden edging, about 9½" x 13" (found in five-and-ten-cent store), white glue, one set Double Six dominoes (if dominoes measure about ⅞" x 1⅞", you need 22), scissors, 40" of white velvet cord, 48" of ½"-wide black velvet ribbon, self-adhesive picture hanger

1. Glue dominoes onto front of wooden frame. They can be arranged as shown—five on each short end, six on each long end—or any other way you prefer. Dominoes run lengthwise along frame. Let glue dry thoroughly. This may take 2 hours or more.

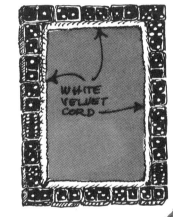

2. Spread a line of glue around the inside edge of frame, between dominoes and blackboard. Press white velvet cord into glue, beginning and ending cord in the same corner.

3. Spread glue around outside edge of dominoes (arrow) and press on black velvet ribbon, cut to fit.

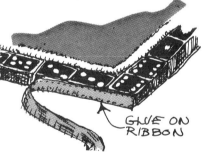

4. Turn frame over, *back side up*, and fasten picture hanger in the middle of the top edge.

THUMBTACK MOSAIC TRIVET

Anyone who can tap a tack with a hammer will have fun creating this easy-to-make gift, which protects a table top from hot pots. Whether you use a piece of scrap lumber or a new board, the finished trivet will be attractive when decorated with its thumbtack mosaic.

Materials: Wood board ½" to 1" thick, any suitable shape and size (such as 5" x 8" rectangle, 6" to 8" circle or square), jigsaw or coping saw (optional), pencil with hard lead, scissors, masking tape, sandpaper, wood stain or clear shellac or enamel or acrylic paint and brush, three to five packages of colored thumbtacks (number needed depends on size of board and your design), hammer

1. If your wood is approximately the right size and shape, plan the design of your mosaic to fit it. If you prefer a different shape, plan it on paper, cut shape out, and tape it onto the wood. Draw around outlines. Remove paper. **With help or permission of an adult,** use saw to cut out wood.

2. Use sandpaper to smooth the wood. Use stain, shellac, or paint on front, sides, and back. Let wood dry several hours or overnight.

3. While finish is drying, plan mosaic design on paper. Tape the paper with the mosaic design on top of the finished wood. Draw around design lines with hard lead pencil, pressing firmly to transfer shapes. Remove paper.

TAPED PAPER

WOOD

4. Fill in the areas of your design with colored thumbtacks placed as close together as possible. First press tacks into wood by hand, then lightly tap them with a hammer. Edges can be tacked or left plain.

HAMMER TACKS

SHEEPSKIN SHOE BUFFER

This shoe polisher is made quickly and easily from a small scrap of sheepskin and leather thongs.

Materials: Sheepskin (piece approximately 3″ x 14″ with fur on one side, leather on the other), ruler, chalk, scissors, old magazine, hammer, nail, two 16″ leather thongs or bootlaces

1. Place piece of sheepskin *leather side up* on table. Use ruler and chalk to measure and mark outlines of a long rectangle, approximately 3″ x 14″. It can be longer or wider, depending on shape of your piece of sheepskin. Cut out shape with scissors and round off the corners.

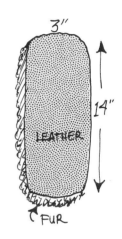

2. Set sheepskin *leather side up* on top of old magazine. Hammer two nail holes about 1″ apart near each end of the piece, as shown. Remove nail.

3. Cut two 16″ leather thongs. Use point of nail to push a thong through each pair of holes, from the fur side out to the leather side. Pull thong until ends are even, then tie ends together in overhand knot as shown.

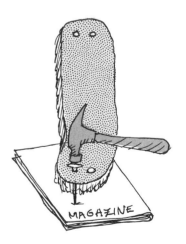

4. To use buffer, place it fur side down on shoe or boot and pull back and forth on leather handles.

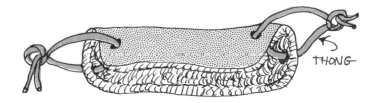

CANDLE

CANDLE
HOLDER

SHELF
SPACER

WOOD
SPINDLE

FLAT
FENCE POST
CAPS

WOOD CANDLESTICKS AND DOLLS

You may have seen a display of unfinished wood furniture legs, spindles, and fence posts in a hardware store, but you may not have realized you were looking at a rich source of inexpensive candlesticks and dolls. Imagination and paint can coax unexpected personality from any turned piece of wood, making it into a very creative gift.

Materials: Unfinished wood elements (such as spindles, shelf spacers, fence post tops and flat caps, table legs and spacers, and drapery pole finials; these come in many shapes and sizes and are found in hardware and building supply stores), sketch paper, pencil, scrap wood or fence post cap or cork (for base), white glue, sandpaper, shellac and brush, acrylic or enamel paint and brush, candle holders (many types are available in hobby and craft shops and in candle shops that sell candle-making supplies. For example, there are heavy brass or iron holders with a screw or screw hole in the bottom, made to hold ½″ or standard ⅞″ tapers. Other commercial holders are made of a pliable brass or tin cup tacked to a flat base. The cup can be pried off the base and thumbtacked on top of the candlestick. Or you can use a wooden holder made for birthday candles, or a Christmas tree candle holder), pliers or tinsnips (if needed, step 4), screw or tack (optional), felt or sheet cork, candle

ELF

FINIALS

SOLDIER DOLL

1. Select a wood shape and study it to see what form it suggests. Let the shape itself dictate its character. A fat 12″ spindle might make a fine geometrically painted candlestick as shown at left; a gracefully curved 15″ table leg might suggest a fat-bellied candlestick man in a waistcoat; a curved, cone-topped finial could become an elf's head or a soldier doll.

Copy the shape of your piece on sketch paper. Within this outline, plan your design—whether realistic or abstract.

37

2. For stability, glue a wide flat base on the bottom of your piece before decorating it. The base can be scrap wood, a flat ¾" fence post cap, or—for finials—an ordinary cork of the same diameter, glued on wide side down.

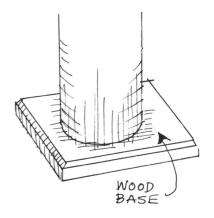

WOOD BASE

3. Use sandpaper to smooth all wood surfaces. Seal wood with a coat of shellac. When shellac is dry, sketch design directly onto wood with pencil. Paint design, covering large background areas and base first. When dry, paint on details. Let paint dry thoroughly; this may take several hours or overnight. In damp weather, enamels may take a day or two to dry.

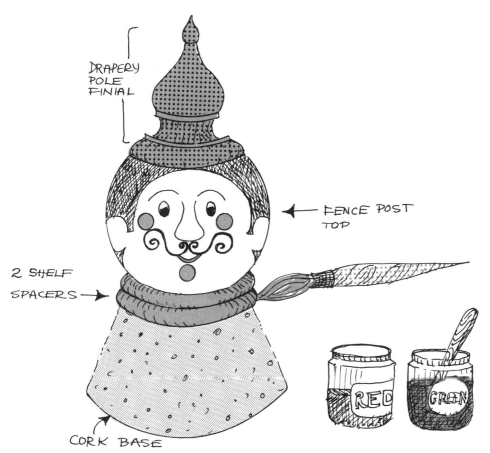

DRAPERY POLE FINIAL

FENCE POST TOP

2 SHELF SPACERS →

CORK BASE

RED GREEN

4. Prepare candle holder to fit on top of candlestick. If you are using a Christmas tree candle holder, bend or cut away unwanted parts of holder with pliers or tinsnips (a). If your holder is a cup shape tacked to a flat base, you may leave it as is and glue it to top of candlestick; if base is too large, use tinsnips to cut it smaller, or simply pry base off (b) and thumbtack cup directly onto candlestick. Paint candle holder to match design, or leave it plain. Attach holder to top of candlestick with screw (c), tack, or glue.

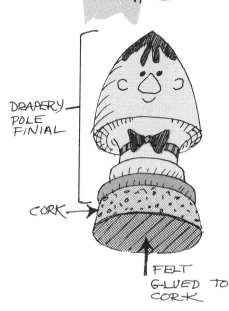

a
CHRISTMAS TREE CANDLE HOLDER

CUT AWAY TREE GRIPPER CLIP

b
CUP
PRY OFF BASE

c
CANDLE HOLDER WITH SCREW

SET INTO CANDLE-STICK

DRAPERY POLE FINIAL

CORK →

FELT GLUED TO CORK

5. To complete candlestick or doll, cover its base with a glued-on piece of felt or sheet cork.

Before gift wrapping candlestick, select and include a candle that complements its color and design. Tall holders look good with medium to tall tapered or straight-sided candles; broad stocky bases look good with thick straight-sided candles, either tall or short.

PATCHWORK FLOWERPOTS

Découpage ordinary flowerpots with patches of gay fabric to make quick, unique gifts for anyone who loves plants. If you wish, you can put plants in the pots before giving them away.

Materials: Flowerpot (clay or plastic; or wide-mouth jar or plastic food-storage container), scissors, fabric (brightly colored cotton calico or other nonbulky fabric; or use colored papers such as gift wrap or pictures cut from magazines), white glue, clear varnish or découpage varnish or clear shellac and brush (optional)

1. Be sure flowerpot or other container is clean and dry inside and out. Cut pieces of fabric or paper of different sizes and colors. Overlap and glue pieces down all over pot. Fold over and glue down pieces on inside rim to a depth of about ½″. Also glue pieces onto bottom surface of pot. If pot has a drainage hole in bottom, do not cover it. Trim any hanging threads.

2. When glue is dry, brush on a coat of varnish or shellac. (You can make your own "varnish" from white glue thinned with water; it will be clear when dry.) Varnish the inside of a terra cotta clay pot as well as the outside, to keep moisture from seeping through to the decorated surface. After the first coat is dry, brush on a second coat to give a glossy finish. Be sure varnish is thoroughly dry (at least overnight) before gift wrapping pot. To gift wrap pot containing plant, see page 95.

GARDENING GLOVES

Gardening is hard on the hands, and gloves—especially personally decorated ones—are a welcome and luxurious gift for any gardener.

Materials: Sturdy, solid-colored cloth gloves (find out the correct size to fit your gardener), sketch paper, pencil, waterproof (oil-base) felt-tip pens or acrylic or oil paint and brush or felt and fabric scraps and needle and embroidery thread

1. Set both gloves, *backs up,* on sketch paper and draw around them. Inside these outlines, sketch designs for glove trimming.

2. Make flowers (your gardener's favorites, if you know them) and leaves for each fingertip. Use felt-tip pens, paints, or bits of felt or fabric sewn in place. Draw or sew on flower stems. Make a painted or sewn fabric flowerpot or bouquet bow at the wrist. For an added personal touch, include the gardener's name in the design.

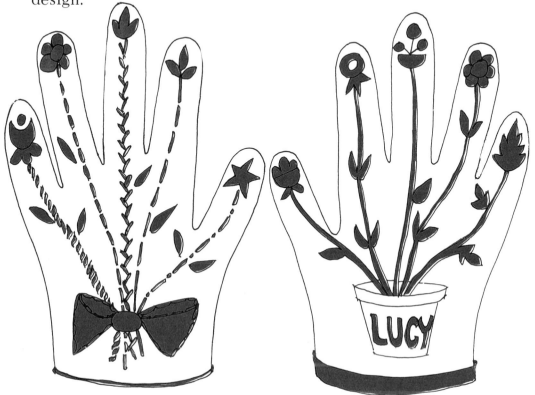

BEAN SPROUTER

Did you know that in less than a week you could grow vitamin-packed, delicious plants in your own kitchen? Dry beans and seeds, kept in a container and rinsed with water, send out shoots in three to five days. It is fascinating to watch the sprouts grow, and they are a delicious and healthful food.

To make a delightful, imaginative, and inexpensive gift for anyone of any age, copy the **bold face** instructions below on a piece of colored paper. (The information in regular type is of general interest but is not essential. Copy it only if you wish to.) Along with the instructions, give a glass quart jar for a sprouter, a piece of cheesecloth, a rubber band, and a ¼-pound packet of dry beans.

Materials: Sprouter (the simplest is an empty, clean quart-size glass jar with a wide mouth. Sprouters also can be made of glass or unglazed pottery jars or bowls or deep-sided dishes), measuring cup, dry beans or seeds (the easiest to sprout are mung beans; try them first. You can also sprout soybeans, peas, lentils, wheat or rye kernels, alfalfa seeds, and nearly every other dry edible bean or seed you can think of. Buy beans and seeds in a health food store or Oriental grocery, and ask for edible sprouting seeds. Do not use seeds sold for planting, which may have been treated with pesticides), strainer, drinking water, double-layered cheesecloth or a clean piece of old nylon stocking (a 6″ to 8″ square will cover the top of a quart jar—use a larger piece for the top of a larger sprouter), rubber band

1. **For 4 cups of full-grown sprouts, measure about ¼ cup beans or seeds into a saucepan or sprouter jar. Rinse with water and pick out any cracked or broken pieces. Drain in a strainer. Return beans to pot or jar, cover with at least 2 cups water, and let stand overnight.**

Beans will absorb some of the water and will swell to almost twice their original size.

2. The next morning, drain beans in a strainer. Place them in sprouter jar and cover top of jar with cheesecloth or nylon fastened with rubber band.

3. For three to five days, rinse the sprouts every morning and evening. Place covered jar under faucet and fill jar with cool water. Then turn jar upside down and drain out all water. **SPROUTS SHOULD BE KEPT DAMP BUT NEVER WET: ALWAYS DRAIN OUT WATER AFTER RINSING.** Store jar in cupboard or on counter top.

DRAINED SPROUTS

If jar is left in sunlight, sprout leaves will turn dark green because chlorophyll will develop; sprouts grown in a dark place will be lighter in color.

If sprouts sit in water too long, they will rot or turn sour; if this happens, you can tell by their smell. Throw bad sprouts away and try again, following directions carefully. If sprouts seem too dry (this may happen in very hot weather), rinse them three times a day.

4. Most sprouts are ready to eat when they are slightly longer than their dry beans. Mung beans are generally eaten after four days, when they are around 2″ to 2½″ long. Eat the entire sprout—bean, attached roots, stem, leaves, and bean casing. Experiment to see what length sprout you prefer.

CASING

5. When sprouts are ready to eat, rinse and drain them, then store them in a plastic bag or other closed container in the refrigerator. They will stay fresh up to ten days.

Eat raw sprouts as a snack right from the refrigerator, or serve them in sandwiches (try peanut butter and sprouts, egg or tuna fish salad and sprouts), green salads, omelettes, scrambled eggs, and hot or cold soups. Add them to pancake batter or to meat loaf, hamburgers, or cooked vegetables.

PAPER BEADS

Paper beads are very easy and quick to make and are especially fun for a rainy day project.

Materials: Colored paper (any flexible paper such as gift wrap, magazine pictures, or plain typewriter paper which can be decorated; amount of paper needed depends on number of beads—an 8″ x 9″ sheet makes 15 beads each 1″ wide), felt-tip pens or crayons or paints (to decorate plain paper), ruler, pencil, scissors, white glue or rubber cement, long thin rod (approximately ⅛″ diameter, such as #2 knitting needle or thin nail), shellac and brush, darning needle and button thread or clear nylon fishing line (for stringing beads), elastic thread or earring backs (optional)

1. If your paper is not decorated, paint or color one side of it with brightly colored patterns. Use all-over patterns with swirled colors or stripes; detailed designs will not show when beads are rolled up.

2. Beads are made from long paper triangles which are spread with glue, then rolled up over a thin rod. The size of the bead depends on the size of the paper triangle. It is fun to make a variety of sizes. An average-size, well-rounded bead is made from a triangle 1″ wide at the base and 9″ long. Triangles can be cut freehand, or measured any size you want. In either case, cut the long legs of the triangle of equal length. If the triangle leans to one side, it will make a very uneven bead when it is rolled up.

EVEN UNEVEN

3. Spread newspaper on work surface. To make a bead, set one triangle *wrong side up* on the newspaper and cover it with glue. Place rod or needle across wide base end (a) and roll paper tightly over it toward the tip (b), which should be centered on the bead as shown. Be sure tip is well glued down, then slide bead off rod (c) and set it to dry.

4. To protect beads and give them added strength, paint them with shellac and let them dry thoroughly.

5. Cut a length of button thread or nylon line and thread it through a darning needle. Make a large knot in one end of the thread; knot must be bigger than holes in beads, so they cannot slide off the end. String beads. When necklace length is reached, remove needle and tie ends of thread together with several strong knots. Cut off extra thread.

6. You can make bracelets by stringing beads on elastic thread. To make hanging earrings, string a single bead on a thin piece of wire or nylon line and fasten it to the hanging loop on an earring (a). Repeat for second earring. Several beads of varying sizes, some of them very large, can be fastened together on a wire or thread, then hung from a chain, making a pendant (b).

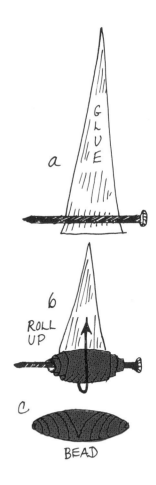

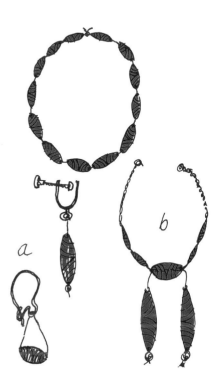

FELT ROSEBUDS

You will delight your friends and surprise yourself with how easily you can make these fanciful felt rosebuds. Add a pin and you have a boutonnière to wear on a lapel; add a bobby pin and rosebud can be worn in the hair. Wrap a ribbon-held lace or paper doily around a cluster of buds to make a nosegay, or fasten several buds to a single stem to make a budding branch for a party table or centerpiece.

Materials: Flexible stem wire (such as medium-weight #15 wire sold for paper flowers), wire cutters, ruler, pliers (optional), #2 or #32 spool wire, brightly colored felt or cotton or silk (green plus other bright colors), chalk or pencil, scissors, rubber cement, florist's tape (found in hobby or flower shops). *For centerpiece:* Small flowerpot, colored paper or thin cardboard, modeling clay or Styrofoam

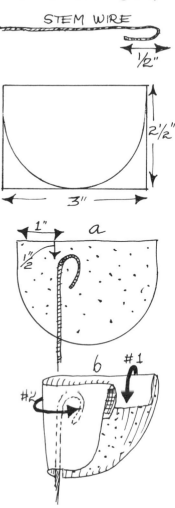

1. To make a stem for one rosebud, cut a piece of stem wire as long as you want it to be; our example is 6″ long. Use pliers if necessary to bend a ½″ loop in one end of the wire. Also cut two pieces of spool wire, each about 5″ long.

2. To make a rosebud, cut a 2½″ x 3″ piece of felt; trim three sides into a curve as shown.

3. Set bud felt flat on table, straight edge on top. Spread rubber cement (dotted area) all over it. Press on the stem wire—loop up—about 1″ over from left side and ½″ below top edge (a). Then fold down ½″ of top edge, covering loop (b, arrow #1). Fold left edge of felt over onto the wire and press flat (b, arrow #2). With thumb and forefinger of one hand, pinch felt together and hold it just below loop while other hand wraps top right cor-

ner across front and down toward stem (arrow, c), sandwiching flap inside and shaping bud. Pinch base of bud together and fasten it with a twisted-on piece of spool wire (d).

4. To make leaf calyx, cut a 2½" x 2" piece of green felt; measure and mark a line ½" up from bottom long edge. Above this line, draw and cut out three pointed leaves, as shown.

5. Brush rubber cement over bud base and wrapped spool wire. Wrap calyx strip around bud as shown, leaves pointing up, and use second piece of spool wire to fasten calyx to bud.

6. Cut a 10" length of florist's tape. To complete bud, cover entire base of bud with tape. Hold one end of the tape onto the calyx wire while pulling the rest of the tape around and wrapping it over itself several times. Tape will stick to itself if you stretch and overlap it as you wind it all the way down the stem.

7. To make a branch of rosebuds for a party table centerpiece, make six to ten rosebuds as described above. Set a small flowerpot, top down, on a piece of colored paper or thin cardboard. Draw around pot (a); ⅛" *inside* drawn lines, cut out circle. Cut a 10" length of stem wire. Use florist's tape to fasten the buds in an evenly spaced arrangement around the wire (b). Glue a piece of modeling clay or Styrofoam into the bottom of the flowerpot. Poke bottom of stem wire through center of paper circle, then stick stem into clay or Styrofoam in bottom of pot, as shown. Slide paper circle down stem.

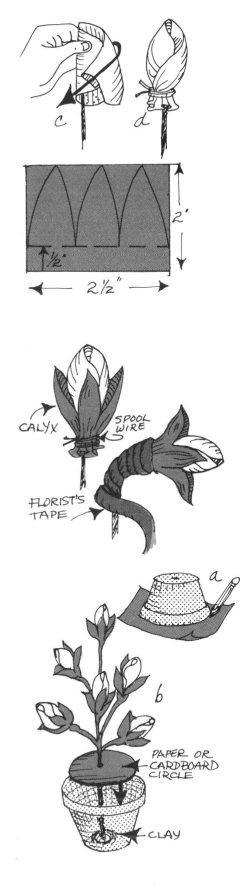

DRIED FLOWER NOTE CARDS

You can quickly transform plain store-bought note cards into one-of-a-kind treasures by gluing on dried grasses, flowers, leaves, or ferns. A box of trimmed cards makes a unique and thoughtful gift for anyone who loves nature.

Materials: Dried plants (flowers, leaves, grasses, ferns), old magazine, heavy books, tweezers, note cards (solid color or white, boxed with matching envelopes), white glue or rubber cement, toothpick

1. Gather plants whenever you find them during the year. Place your collection flat between the pages of an old magazine and press it under heavy books. Leave them a week or two until dry. Save dried plants in the magazine or in envelopes in a box, until you are ready to decorate your cards.

2. Dried plants may cling to the magazine; to remove them, pry them up gently with tweezers. Experiment with different arrangements of plants on the cards. The simpler the design, the prettier. Be sure to leave some writing space.

3. To attach plants, use only a few small drops of glue, spread gently onto the back of the plant. You may find it convenient to dip a toothpick in the glue and dab it on the plant. Press plant down in position on paper.

4. Leave decorated cards spread out until glue is dry. Then stack cards in their original box along with their envelopes. Before gift wrapping, you may want to decorate the box itself and add a note telling where you picked the plants.

HAIR RIBBON OR NECKTIE RACK

This easily made rack can be used to store hair ribbons or necklaces or neckties or belts, or to hold hand towels for guests. Make it a personal gift by painting it someone's favorite color or decorating it to match his or her bedroom.

Materials: Wood curtain rod parts (found in building supply or hardware store: dowel or wooden curtain rod or broom handle 18" long, 1" to 1½" diameter; two wood or metal C-shaped brackets with screws for holding curtain rod against a wall; two decorative wood finials for rod ends—with or without screws for fastening), tape measure, saw, white glue, acrylic or enamel paint or shellac or varnish and brush. *For covering rod (optional):* Felt or cotton velvet, scissors, three rubber bands

1. Measure and saw curtain rod or broom handle the correct length, **with help or permission of an adult.** Ours is 18"; yours can be longer or shorter if you prefer. Glue or screw a finial to each end of rod as shown. Paint rod, finials, and brackets. If you prefer the natural wood, shellac or varnish it for protection.

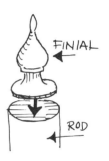

FINIAL

ROD

2. To prevent ribbons or ties from sliding off the rod, you can cover it with a glued-on piece of felt or cotton velvet. To cut fabric to fit around rod, first measure around rod, then add about 1" more for overlap. In our example, width is 4½", length is 18". Spread glue on rod. Fold under about 1" on each short end of fabric, then press it down onto rod, overlapping and gluing its long edges (arrows, a). About 1" of rod will stick out beyond each end of fabric. You can hold fabric in place with rubber bands while glue is drying.

3. When wrapping the rack as a gift, sit the rod in the wall brackets, and be sure to include screws for fastening the brackets to the wall. You might also drape a tie or ribbon over the rod as an extra gift (b).

49

DECORATIVE NOTE PAD

This is a welcome gift for any busy person. The pad and attached pencil, covered with decorative paper, are as festive-looking as they are useful when placed on a desk or hung on the wall beside the telephone.

Materials: New note pad (about 3½" x 6"), cardboard (any stiff board such as mat board, plus a strip of flexible cardboard such as oaktag or shirt cardboard), ruler, X-Acto or utility knife, decorative paper (any pretty paper—one you have painted or printed yourself or gift wrap or wallpaper scraps), scissors, white glue or rubber cement, self-adhesive picture hanger or 4" of string and 3" of adhesive tape or cloth Mystik tape, old magazine, hammer and nail, cotton string or yarn, new pencil

1. To make a backing board, measure and cut out a piece of stiff cardboard at least ½" larger all around than your note pad. In our example, the pad is 3½" x 6"; the cardboard is 5" x 7".

2. To cover the backing board, cut a piece of decorative paper 1" larger than your board. In example, paper is 6" x 8". Cut off corners of paper as shown (a). Place paper *wrong side up* on table. Spread glue all over paper and on one side of board; center board over paper, then press glued sides together. Pull edges of paper over (b), gluing them onto the board.

3. To make a hanging strip, cut a ½"-wide strip of flexible cardboard 2" longer than the *width* of your backing board (in example, 5" plus 2" = 7"). Cut a piece of matching decorative paper large enough to wrap around both sides of this strip (about 1¼" x 7"). Spread glue all over strip, then cover it with the paper. Trim off any uneven edges.

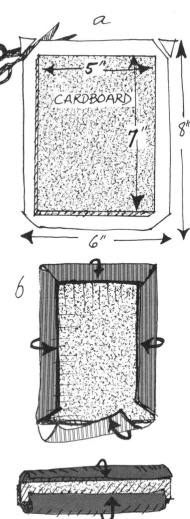

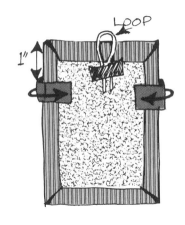

4. To attach the hanging strip to the board, place strip flat on the table. Place the board *wrong side up* on top of it. Bend ends of hanging strip over and glue them firmly onto the back of the board, about 1" below top edge as shown (arrows).

5. If you do not have a self-adhesive picture hanger, make a loop out of a 4" piece of string; fasten it with adhesive or Mystik tape to the center top of the board as shown. If you have a self-adhesive hanger, attach it in step 6.

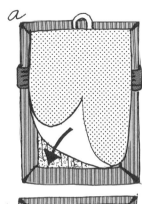

6. To cover the back of the board with decorative paper, set board on the wrong side of a piece of paper and draw around it. Cut slightly *inside* the drawn lines. In example, paper is about 4¾" x 6¾". Spread glue on back of board, then press on paper (a). If you have made a string hanging loop (step 5), it sticks out above paper as shown. If not, fasten a self-adhesive picture hanger onto center top of covering paper (b).

7. Mark a light pencil dot on the front of the covered board, about ½" from the lower right corner. Place board on old magazine, then hammer the nail through marked dot to make a neat hole in the board. Remove nail. Cut a 12" length of string or yarn and tie one end through this hole. Keep knot on back of board. Cover pencil with matching paper. Tie onto string.

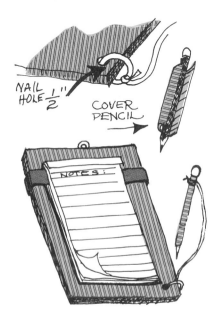

8. To complete, slip the stiff back layer, or last few pages, of the pad over the hanging strip.

DESK ORGANIZER

This gift is a necessity for anyone with a cluttered desk or work area. Scrap boxes are covered, trimmed, and fastened together into a decorative and efficient unit to hold such things as paper clips, rubber bands, pencils, and stamps, or sewing thread, pins, measuring tape, and buttons. Before giving them away, you might fill a few of the boxes with appropriate items.

Materials: Cardboard boxes (various sizes and shapes such as empty note card boxes; pint, quart, and half-gallon milk cartons; and small box lids with sturdy edges), scissors, tempera or acrylic paint and brush, white glue or rubber cement, colored paper (such as gift wrap, newspaper, colored magazine illustrations), tape measure, felt-tip pens or crayons, colored plastic or cloth Mystik tape or fabric ribbon ½″ to 1″ wide, clear shellac or découpage varnish and brush (optional)

1. Remove box tops. Set boxes side by side and experiment with various arrangements. Combine boxes and lids of different heights and shapes. Use scissors to cut off boxes at the height you want. Do not glue boxes together yet.

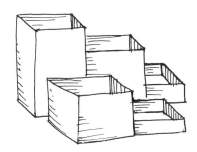

2. To decorate the boxes, paint the inside of each with tempera or acrylic paint and set it aside until dry. (Use acrylic paint or waterproof felt-tip pens to color milk cartons.) Then cover the outside of each container with glued-on strips of colored paper. Wrap a tape measure, or the paper itself, around the outside of the box to measure it before cutting the paper.

You can use the same paper for all the boxes, or make each one different. For example, make a collage by cutting out and pasting down magazine pictures, or cover boxes with stock quotations or a crossword puzzle from a newspaper, or trim boxes with the funny papers or with pages of your old drawings. You can, if you like, label each container (PENCILS, STAMPS) with felt-tip pens, paints, or crayons, or cut-out pieces of colored tape.

3. To make neat edges at the top of each box, trim them with lengths of colored tape or ribbon. Select trimming in a color that goes well with decoration on box. To determine length of trim, wrap tape measure around edge of box. If using ribbon, glue it onto the edge. For tape, wrap it around the box top as shown, pressing half the width onto the outside edge. Make a short cut (arrows) in each corner of the tape, from its top edge down to the top edge of the box. Then press the tape sections over onto the inside surface of the box.

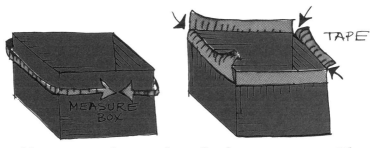

4. Set decorated boxes together in their final arrangement. Glue all touching sides together. Leave arrangement standing flat on table until glue is completely dry. If you like, add strips of trim around bottom edges of boxes.

53

MACRAMÉ PLANT HANGER

This is the simplest possible macramé design. It requires no special skill except one you already have: the ability to tie an ordinary overhand knot. If you happen to have pretty beads, you can tie them on the cords, but even the plainest twine will make a decorative hanger for anyone who enjoys plants. You may want to give a potted plant along with your hanger.

This hanger, with a pot inside, measures about 28″ long from top loop to base fringe. It is scaled to a regular terra cotta flowerpot about 5″ to 5½″ tall. However, the hanger will stretch to fit many other pot sizes or shapes.

Materials: Four 8½′ or 9½′ strands of cord ⅛″ to 3⁄16″ thick (two-ply sisal twine or #48 nylon macramé braid or cord or four-ply jute wrap or cotton cord or leather thong, or any other nonbulky rope or string), tape measure, scissors, protruding nail in board or wall on which to hook cords while knotting, sixteen beads ½″ long with holes large enough for two strands of cord to pass through (optional; if you don't have beads, make extra knots instead)

1. If you plan to combine beads with knots, cut four 8½′ cords; if using all knots without beads, cut four 9½′ cords.

Fold each of the four cords in half and set them side by side. Gather all center loops together and hold them in one hand while straightening out all hanging ends with the other hand. About 3″ below the top of the center loops, tie all the strands into a neat overhand knot as shown. Hook this loop over a nail or other sturdy holder.

2. Take two side-by-side strands of cord, measure along them 4″ below the first knot (#1), and tie them together into overhand knot #2. Repeat with each pair of side-by-side strands, four knots in all.

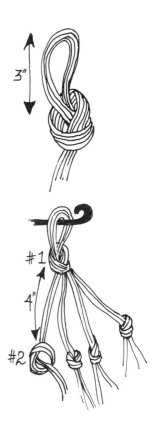

3. If you are using beads, string one onto each pair of strands just below the knot. Push bead up tight against knot, then tie another overhand knot below it (#3). If you are not using beads, tie a middle knot and then knot #3 as shown.

4. Four inches below each knot #3, repeat steps 2 and 3, making knots #4 and #5 on either side of a bead (or a middle knot) on each pair of strands.

5. To make the webbing, take one strand from each of two side-by-side pairs and tie them together 4″ below knot #5 into overhand knot #6. String a bead onto this pair of strands (or make a middle knot), then tie overhand knot #7 just below bead to hold it. Repeat this three more times, using one strand from each of two side-by-side pairs to tie knots with a bead or middle knot in between as shown.

6. Four inches below knot #7, repeat step 5, knotting together one strand from each of two side-by-side pairs (knot #8), adding a bead or middle knot, and then tying another knot (#9).

7. To complete, gather all loose strands together about 3″ or 4″ below the last knot (#9). Tie strands into one single overhand knot (#10). The remaining strands will all hang down in a loose fringe. Trim the ends off evenly.

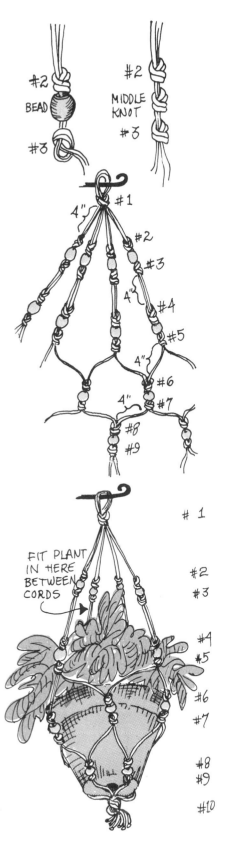

FANCY PIN CUSHION

Once you see pins displayed this way, you will wonder why they are ever hidden away in a jewelry box.

Materials: Container (goblet-shaped vase made of metal, plastic, wood, china, or thick glass; or any other bowl, glass, or vase with attractive shape), enamel or acrylic paint and brush, Styrofoam ball with the same (or nearly the same) diameter as top of container (for a 5″ to 6″ container, use a 5″ ball), X-Acto or utility knife, ruler, fabric (such as cotton, cotton velvet, felt, or lace sewn over a plain piece of any other fabric; an 11″ circle is enough to cover half a 5″ ball for one pin cushion), scissors, straight pins, white glue, hairpin or paper clip, trimming (such as yarn, lace, ribbon, or press-on self-adhesive decorative trim sold in fabric stores)

1. Paint the outside of your container with enamel or acrylic paint, unless it is attractive as it is and you prefer to leave it plain. A transparent container looks better painted.

2. Set the Styrofoam ball in your container. If it fits as shown (a), with half the ball sticking up like ice cream in a cone, then leave the ball whole. If it sticks up too far, then cut the ball in half with a knife. **Be sure you have an adult's help or permission when using the knife.** In our example, we use a ball cut in half, but the method is basically the same for a whole ball.

Set the half ball in the container. If it slides down inside, cut a small block from the other half of the ball and glue it in the bottom of the container to support the ball as shown (b).

3. Cut a circle of fabric large enough to wrap around entire ball or half ball. For half a 5″ ball, cut an 11″ circle of fabric. Set fabric *wrong side up* on table. Set ball *cut side (bottom) up* in center of fabric. Pull opposite edges of fabric over onto the ball as shown, and pin them down. Press pins through fabric all the way into the Styrofoam. Then pull up, overlap, and pin remaining fabric edges, so ball is as smooth as possible on top.

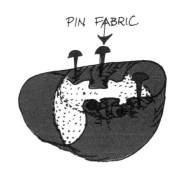

PIN FABRIC

4. If you are using a supporting block inside container, cover top of block with glue. Spread a line of glue around top inside edge of container as shown (a). Then gently but firmly push covered ball, *top up,* into container, where it will be held by the glued edge and the supporting block. Use a hairpin or paper clip to tuck in any loose fabric folds (b).

a
GLUE
b HAIRPIN

5. Glue decorative trim around top edge of container, as shown, hiding the glued rim of the covered ball. Glue additional trim on the base of the container, if you like. Before gift wrapping the pin cushion, you might stick a pin in the top as a small bonus gift.

YARN-COVERED GIFTS
Box, Yarn Painting, Frame or Wreath, Flowerpot, Jewelry Box, Hand Mirror

Brightly colored yarn and a bit of glue can turn ordinary inexpensive objects into the most delightful assortment of creative gifts. Cover a box, hand mirror, flowerpot, or scrap of wood, and suddenly you have an elegant jewelry box, vanity table mirror, pencil or plant holder, or wall plaque. There is no limit to the type or number of gifts you can design by "drawing" with yarn.

Materials: Object to cover: flat scrap of wood, hand mirror, nearly any type of container (flowerpot; cardboard, plastic, or wood box with or without lid; bath powder or hair curler box, hat box, cigar box; round or rectangular cans open at one end—those that hold coffee, oatmeal, or tea), tempera or acrylic or enamel paint and brush, felt-tip pen or crayon, felt, chalk (for marking felt), scissors, plastic squeeze bottle of white glue (the type that dries clear), wool or acrylic yarn (or, for a more tailored look, try rope, twine, or macramé string; you can dye white cotton string beige by soaking it in strong tea or coffee), hairpin, darning needle, or straightened paper clip, clear shellac and brush (optional), straight pin

BOX

1. Select object to be decorated with yarn (or string or rope). Our first example is a yarn-covered box, although the basic instructions in steps 1, 2, and 3 apply to any container or other object.

Study shape of box and plan trimming to complement it. Keep shapes simple. Consider the type of yarn or other material you are going to use. Medium or thin yarn can be formed into small, fairly detailed shapes, while thick, bulky yarn is best for bold forms. Experiment with different designs on sketch paper.

BULKY YARN

THIN YARN

BULKY AND THIN

Glued-on strips of felt can be used in many ways: as part of the design; as covering for sides, edges, or bottom of a box; as container lining; or as a picture frame (see examples following).

2. You may want to paint the inside of a box or container to make it more attractive. Use any type of paint on a cardboard surface, and anything *except* tempera on a metal or plastic or wax-coated surface. Let paint dry well. Or you may prefer to line the box.

3. Draw outlines of your design directly on box or other object, using felt-tip pen or crayon. Plan to glue on felt strips first if you are using them, then cover the main outlines of your design with yarn.

To measure the correct length of each piece of yarn, hold it in position against the box, note the length, and cut it off (a).

To attach the yarn, squeeze a line of glue directly on box over drawn outline (b). Work in one small area at a time. Press yarn into glue. Use a hairpin, darning needle, or paper clip to poke unruly edges and cut ends in place; add extra dabs of glue where necessary to hold yarn. Don't worry if glue shows—it will be invisible when it dries. After the main outlines of design are covered with yarn (c), fill in all background areas with pieces of yarn cut to fit the space, then glued in place. Cover box completely (d).

4. To make a protective cover for bottom of box, set box on a piece of felt. Draw around it with chalk, then cut felt out. Glue felt on bottom of box.

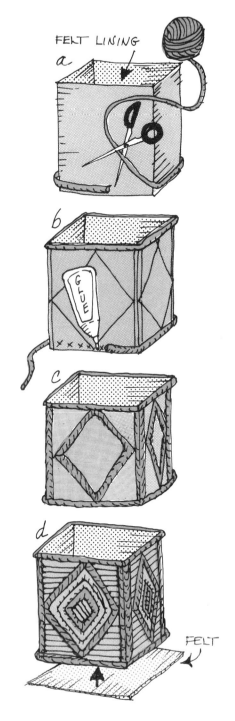

FELT LINING

a

b

c

d

FELT

59

YARN PAINTING

Make an abstract design, write a name, or "paint" a picture—with yarn glued to a piece of wood or stiff cardboard. If you glue a piece of fabric or burlap over your cardboard, yarn design can leave some of the background area exposed. Make frame with strips of felt glued onto front surface; cover edges of backing board with yarn. Hang with self-adhesive picture hanger pressed on back.

FRAME OR WREATH

Wrap yarn, twine, or macramé string around a rectangular or circular frame made from any material, such as wood, Styrofoam, or cardboard. Use a solid-color yarn, or wrap with sections of different colors to create a striped effect. To fasten yarn on back side, slip loose end under several wrapped strands. To prevent background from showing through, wrap strands tightly together. If background shows, glue on extra strands of yarn wherever needed to fill in spaces. To make a framed mirror, glue a lightweight mirror to back of frame. To make wreath, tie a large bow on wrapped circular frame.

FLOWERPOT

Cover outside surface of a flowerpot with yarn, string, or medium-weight rope. Paint string or rope with clear shellac to make a waterproof surface. Do not paint inside of pot, and do not cover its bottom surface with felt.

JEWELRY BOX

Make jewelry box from an oval-shaped plastic box (the type sold in five-and-ten-cent stores for holding hair curlers), a round bath powder box, or a cigar box or other rectangular box. First paint the inside of lid and inner sides of box with gold enamel. When paint is dry, glue strips of felt around outside edge of lid and around exterior sides of box (a).

Cover bottom of box on inside and outside with felt as in step 4, page 59.

To make a flower on top of lid, draw on basic design as shown (b). Glue yarn around outside edge of lid; then add a separate piece of yarn for outline of each petal (c). Between and inside petals, fill in the background with short pieces of contrasting-color yarn (d). On flower's center, glue on large spiral of yarn. Spiral should cover the inside edge of each petal. Hold end of spiral in position with pin until glue is dry. To complete, glue one or two rows of flower-colored yarn around outside bottom edge of box (e).

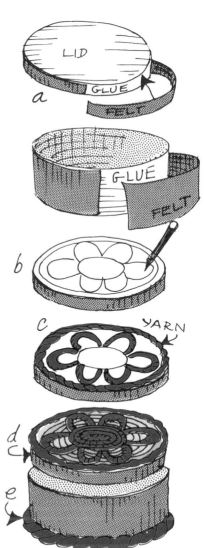

61

HAND MIRROR

Cover front and back sides of a hand mirror with felt trimmed with yarn. First pin together two layers of felt. Place mirror on top layer and draw around it with chalk (a). About ⅛" outside drawn line, cut out shape. Remove pins. Use scissors point to poke a center hole in round end of one felt piece, then enlarge hole into a circle approximately the size of mirror glass (b). Glue this piece of felt on mirror front. Glue second piece of felt (without hole) on back. Pinch both glued layers of felt together all around outside edges (c). If edges are uneven, trim them with scissors after glue is dry. Decorate back of mirror with design such as yarn flower (d), following directions for Jewelry Box, page 61, steps b-d. To complete, glue a narrow yarn border around edge of mirror glass (e). Omit this border if your mirror is very small.

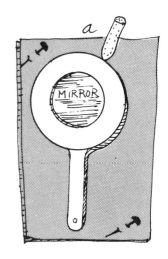

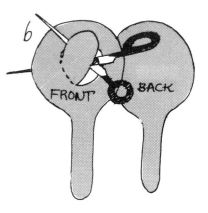

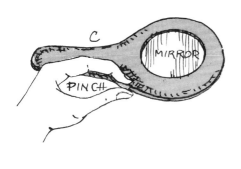

LAP DESK

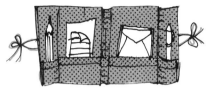

A lap desk is a handy gift for anyone who writes letters. It is especially convenient for a traveler, because it is both a portable writing surface and a carrying case for stationery and a pen.

Materials: One 22½" x 28" sheet of sturdy colored paper (such as wallpaper, gift wrapping paper, hand-blocked imported paper, or brown wrapping paper previously decorated with painted or printed designs), ruler, scissors, pencil, two 8½" x 11" pieces of lightweight cardboard such as shirt cardboard, rubber cement or white glue, Mystik tape (cloth or plastic, in a color that goes well with your colored paper), old magazine, two thumbtacks, paper clips, stapler that can be opened and used flat, two 16" lengths of narrow ribbon or thin yarn, "write-on" cellophane mending tape

1. Cut colored paper 22½" x 28". Set paper *wrong side up,* with short edges at top and bottom as shown. On top edge, measure and mark point A, 2½" over from left corner. Mark point B, 8½" over from A. Mark C, ½" from B, and D, 8½" from C. Draw dotted line across paper 11" below top edge.

2. Cut two 8½" x 11" pieces of cardboard. Glue the cardboards to the paper as follows: First spread glue across the top 11" of paper (to dotted line). Then spread glue on one side of each piece of cardboard. Line up the short end of one board with edge A-B and press it glued side down. Leave ½" space, then press second glued board between marks C and D in the same manner. Spread more glue on paper (striped areas). Spread glue all over both pieces of cardboard.

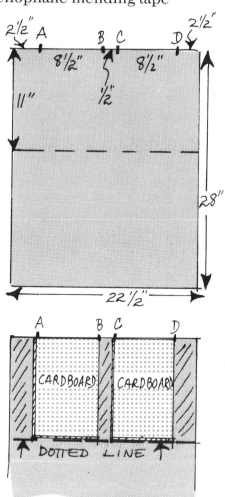

3. Lift up the top edge of paper—with boards attached—and, folding on dotted line, glue it face down onto the paper below it as shown (arrow). Boards are now sandwiched between two paper layers. Smooth out wrinkles by pressing paper firmly down from top toward the bottom. Turn entire piece over and smooth outside surface. Add more glue wherever paper edges lift up from cardboard.

4. Spread glue all over the 6"-high area just below the covered cardboards (see drawing above). Then fold paper's bottom edge up to meet the base of the boards, making a 3"-high flap (a). Press along fold and smooth both layers flat.

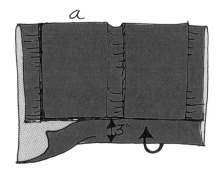

Fold a strip of tape in half over bottom edge of flap. To do this, cut a 22½" length of colored Mystik tape. Set it *sticky side up* on a magazine. Push a thumbtack through each end of tape (b) to hold it flat. Press paper flap onto *half* of tape's width. Remove tacks, then fold remaining tape, pressing it up onto the flap.

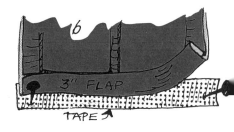

5. The taped flap is now folded over onto the boards (a) to make the pockets. Hold flap in place with a few paper clips. Turn lap desk over with its *outside facing up*. Place one side in stapler as shown (b). Fasten outside edges of flap with staples #1 and #2, running parallel to sides of lap desk (c). Place staples #3 and #4 just before the edge of the nearest cardboard. Place four more staples in opposite end of flap.

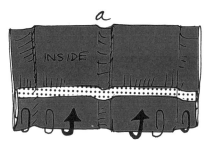

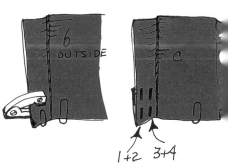

6. Place two more staples (#5 and #6) in the middle of the flap, between the boards. To do this, open the stapler flat. Set lap desk flat *outside up,* on a magazine (a). Position stapler as shown, so staples will be parallel to other staples. Press staples through the paper and into the magazine. Carefully lift lap desk up and turn it over. On the inside, bend staple legs in, pressing them flat with a ruler.

Fold an 11½" piece of colored Mystik tape in half lengthwise over the two outer edges of the side flap (arrows, b). The narrow side pocket of each flap will hold pens or pencils; stationery and envelopes fit in the pockets over the covered cardboards.

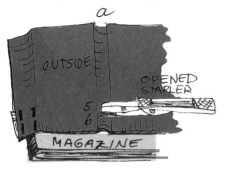

7. For ties, cut two 16" lengths of ribbon or yarn. Open lap desk as in step 6 (b). In each side flap, measure 5" down from the top edge and place a 2" length of "write-on" mending tape alongside the covered cardboard as shown. With scissors or pencil point, poke two small holes in tape, about 1" apart. Use pencil point to carefully push yarn or ribbon ends through these holes from outside to inside. Tie ends together with knot on inside as shown.

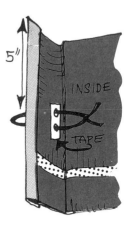

8. To close completed lap desk, fold in side flaps as you would the flaps on a book jacket. Fold the covered boards onto each other and tie ribbons together. When giving lap desk as a gift, place a few sheets of writing paper, envelopes, and a pen or pencil in the pockets.

PETS' CHRISTMAS STOCKINGS

With these stockings hanging by the fireplace, Santa Claus will be sure to remember your pets on Christmas Eve.

Materials: Sketch paper and pencil, large-size old woolen socks or knee socks, scraps of felt or other fabrics, scissors, straight pins, needle and thread or white glue, trimmings such as colored yarn, buttons, beads, etc., waterproof felt-tip pens, or embroidery thread and needle (optional)

1. Copy designs below or make up your own pattern to resemble your pet. Sketch design first on paper.

2. Cut out pieces of felt or fabric. Pin, then sew or glue them down on sock. When sewing, put one hand—or a small empty jar—inside sock to hold the sides apart so they won't be stitched together. When gluing, put a piece of wax paper into sock so glue cannot soak through and fasten sides of sock together. If you like, use felt-tip pens to draw some details, or do embroidery stitches with needle and embroidery thread. Sew on buttons, beads, or other trimming.

SNOUT · CUT FROM ONE PIECE · YARN BRAID · SEWN ON FELT · MOUSE · FILL WITH CATNIP

CATNIP MOUSE

Materials: Sketch paper, pencil, ruler, scissors, straight pins, felt, needle and thread or sewing machine, 6″ length of yarn, catnip

The patterns for mouse's body, ears, and eyes are on page 83. To make paper patterns and cut out pieces, see page 76, steps 2 and 4. To sew mouse together, follow directions on page 77, step 5. Stuff mouse with catnip. Use 6″ length of yarn for tail. Knot end of tail.

PET'S MUNCHIES BOX

This decorative container will hold a good supply of holiday treats for your pet—dog biscuits, cat crunchies, birdseed, or fish food.

Materials: Container (round cardboard or metal oatmeal box or round biscuit tin or metal tea box), tape measure, covering material (self-adhesive paper or construction paper or gift wrap, or felt or other fabric), pencil, scissors, sketch paper, felt-tip pens or crayons or tempera or acrylic paint and brush or colored tape, white glue, hammer and nail (for metal containers), 20″ length of braided or plain yarn or rope

1. Use tape measure to determine height of container; also measure distance around container and add 1″ for overlap. Measure, mark, and cut out paper or fabric this size. (A 1-lb. 2-oz. oatmeal carton is 7¼″ tall, 12¾″ around plus 1″.) To make lid top covering, set lid on another piece of paper or fabric, draw around it, then cut out shape. To cover lid sides, glue on strip of the same paper or fabric.

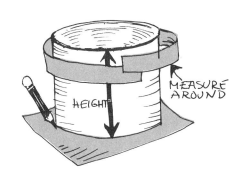

2. Set lid and container covers flat on table and decorate them with any designs you like. Copy these designs or sketch your own—on paper first, then on covers, using crayons, pens, or paints. Or cut designs from colored tape. Spread glue on outside of container, then wrap cover around it and overlap edges. Glue lid cover on top.

3. To make a handle, remove lid from container. Poke two holes in opposite sides of container about 2″ down from top edge. Use pencil to poke holes (pushing from outside to inside) in cardboard, or nail and hammer to make holes in metal. Push ends of yarn or rope through holes from outside to inside and make a large knot in each end. Knots must be big enough to grip on inside of container.

(YOU CAN LEAVE OFF HANDLE IF YOU PREFER)

STRING DISPENSER BOX

This inexpensive and quickly made gift is simply a covered box containing a ball of string which pulls out through a hole in the lid. For cutting the string, attach a small pair of scissors.

Materials: Box with lid, large enough to hold a ball or spool of string (any box at least 4½" on each side will do; for example, an empty greeting card or note card box, or a cardboard oatmeal box. Cut box if sides are too high), ball of string, colored paper, ruler, pencil, scissors, rubber cement, X-Acto knife or utility knife, plastic or cloth Mystik tape in a color that goes well with your colored paper, 10" of ½" grosgrain or other ribbon (optional); small pair of scissors (optional)

1. Set ball of string inside box to be sure it will fit when lid is closed. Remove ball and lid.

Cover bottom of box with colored paper. (Cover lid separately, following the same directions.) Set box in middle of paper and mark box position as shown. On all four sides, measure paper by pulling it up and wrapping it over the edge. Allow an extra ½" for overlap, then cut off paper. On two sides, draw dotted lines from box corners to edge of paper as shown. To make paper fit well, cut notches about ½" deep and ½" wide at outside end of each dotted line.

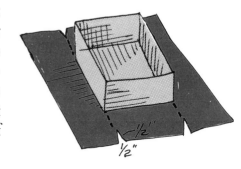

2. Lift box and spread rubber cement all over its bottom and sides. Set it back in place on paper. On sides #1 and #2, fold paper up and over box. Glue edges onto inside surface. Then fold end flaps over (arrows, a) making triangular-shaped folds. Pull these flaps up and glue them against box.

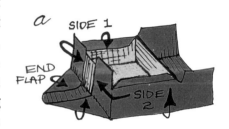

Glue flap edges onto inside of box (b).
3. To cover a round container, see directions for wrapping a cylinder, page 96. Leave one end of container open, and make a flat cover for other end (a). To cover top of round lid, draw around it on colored paper, then cut shape out and glue it down on lid top. Cover lid edge with colored tape. To do this, press bottom half of the tape around the edge (b), cut slits in top half, overlap and fold tape down on top of paper circle.
4. In the center of the lid, cut a slit about 1″ x ¼″, or make a ½″ diameter hole. Use scissors point or knife, **with the help or permission of an adult.** To cover cut edge of hole, wrap a piece of colored tape over it as shown, pressing half the width onto the top surface of the lid and half onto the inside surface. Slit tape to ease around curves.
5. You can add string and consider box complete at this point, or you can add scissors holder as follows. First, put lid on box and make light pencil mark on box just below lid. Remove lid. At this point, use knife or scissors (**with help or permission of an adult**) to make two holes about 2″ apart in middle of box side.

Cut a 10″ length of ½″-wide ribbon. Push each end of ribbon into one hole, pull ends taut on inside of box and tie them in a double knot (a). Tuck scissors into ribbon holder on outside of box. Put string or wire ball in box, pull one end of string through hole in lid as shown (b), then put lid on box.

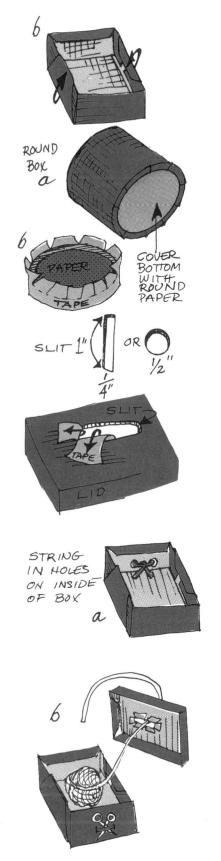

69

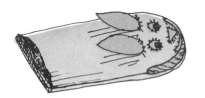
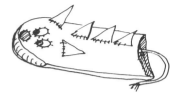

BATH PUPPET

Made entirely of facecloths, this hand puppet can scrub you clean in the tub as easily as he can perform on a puppet stage. Following our basic pattern, you can design any puppet personality you like. This gift is fun for children of every age.

Materials: Two matching brightly colored terry cloth facecloths (or pieces of old towels) each about 12″ x 12″, straight pins, tape measure, chalk or soft lead pencil, scissors, tracing paper, one facecloth of contrasting color the same size, needle and thread or sewing machine, two large buttons or pieces of ball fringe (optional)

1. To make the puppet's top and bottom panels, pin the matching facecloths together, *right sides together*. Measure, mark, and cut both cloths 6½″ wide. If face cloths are approximately 12″ long, leave the ends uncut, as shown; if they are much longer, cut the ends off at 12″. Save scraps for later use.

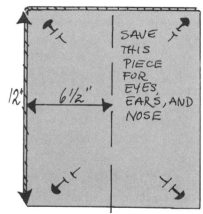

2. Pin both 6½″ x 12″ layers together. Measure and mark a dotted chalk line 3½″ from one end, as shown. Cut this end into a curve as shown, making the puppet's mouth.

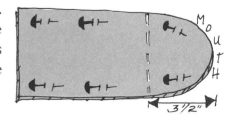

3. Remove any pins between chalk line and curve. Leave remaining pins along the sides. Fold the rounded end of the top layer back on itself as shown. The striped oval area shown is the size of the opened mouth.

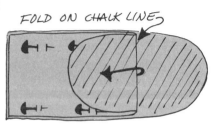

FOLD ON CHALK LINE

4. To make the mouth lining, place a piece of tracing paper on top of the opened mouth and press down with your fingers to feel the edges of the oval shape. Pin the paper to the cloth in a couple of places. Mark the edges of the mouth with chalk or pencil; you should have an oval about 6½" x 7". Remove pins from paper. Cut oval out and pin it on a piece of contrasting-color terry cloth. Cut out the cloth, making the mouth lining (a). Bring short ends of the lining together to fold it in half. Place a pin at each end of the folded edge (b).

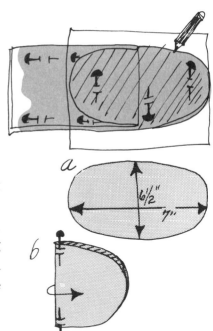

5. To make flat ears, cut out any shapes you like from the terry cloth scraps; sew by hand or by machine around all cut edges to keep them from unraveling.

To make folded ears which will stick up, cut out two triangles as shown (a), using the corners of one of the scraps. Make these triangles as big as you like. In example, each side is 3" long, measured out from the corner along the selvage, or finished, edge. The triangles shown are about 2" deep, measured straight in from corner. With selvage edges pointing up (b), overlap bottom corner points X and Y to make a base about 1½" wide (c). Sew across this base (dotted line). Then turn both ears inside out.

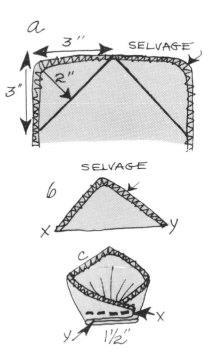

6. Remove pins holding puppet's top and bottom panels together. Place top panel *right side up*. At dotted chalk line, attach each ear to the puppet's body by stitching around the base.

7. To make eyes, cut two ¾″ circles from scrap terry cloth. Eye color should contrast with body color. Eyes can also be made from large buttons or pieces of ball fringe. To make nose, cut out a cloth triangle. Attach all features to the puppet by sewing around them with overcast stitch (page 13) so fabric will not unravel. Add any other decorative details you wish—stripes, spots, tail, etc.

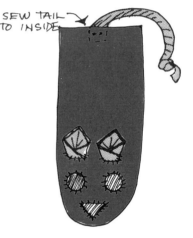

SEW TAIL TO INSIDE

8. To put puppet together, place decorated top panel flat on the table, *right side up*. Pin, then sew on *half* the oval mouth lining made in step 4. To do this, place the lining *wrong side up* on top of the puppet's face, covering it. One of the lining's short ends should line up with the mouth curve. The pins marking the center of each side of the lining should line up with the dotted chalk line on the top panel. These pins also mark where your stitches will begin and end.

    Now pin and sew both pieces together (dotted line). Stitches should be about ¼″ in from edge. Remove pins.

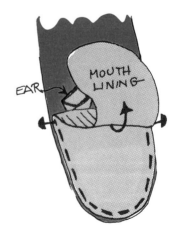

EAR

MOUTH LINING

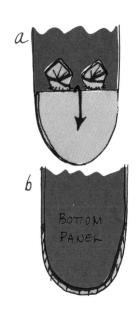

9. Fold over unsewn half of mouth lining onto sewn half (arrow, a). Cover this with the remaining (bottom) panel of body, placed *wrong side up* as shown. Rounded end of panel covers folded mouth lining (b). Grasp both the uppermost body panel and the unsewn lining and pull them over as shown (c); pin their rounded edges together. Then sew pieces together about ¼" in from edges (dotted line, d). Remove pins.

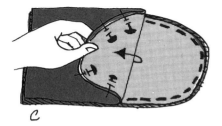

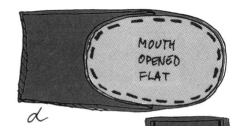

10. Close puppet's mouth. Pin long sides together, then stitch down each long side from the corner of the mouth (arrows) to the end of each side. Remove pins. Trim off any long threads.

11. Turn puppet inside out by reaching inside the open end and carefully pulling the cloth out the opening. To work the puppet, put your hand inside until your fingers feel the ends of his mouth. Put your thumb inside the bottom half of his jaw and your fingers in the top half. When giving the puppet as a gift, you can put a new bar of soap in his mouth before wrapping, to show that the puppet is for the bath as well as for play.

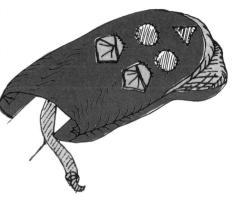

LEARNING PILLOW

Make this decorative pillow for a young child who is very special to you. The designs can teach a toddler letters or numbers, as well as dressing skills—buttoning, tying, snapping, and zipping. Make up your own pattern using any shapes you like, or copy ours. Sew by machine or by hand, using plain or fancy stitches. Although these directions seem rather long, the individual steps are easy to follow, and the results are well worth the extra time. This is a good project for a group to work on together.

Materials: Sketch paper, tape measure, pencil, brightly colored felt (which will not unravel at the edges; felt can be wiped off with water but is not completely washable) or washable fabric (any sturdy weave such as cotton or a polyester blend), scissors, straight pins, pillow stuffing (cotton batting or kapok or old clean rags or foam rubber or polyurethane foam), yarn (wool or acrylic—three pieces of medium weight, each 24″ long, and two pieces of bulky weight, each 18″ long), pinking shears (optional), scrap cardboard, X-Acto or utility knife, sewing needle and thread or sewing machine, 5″ zipper (or a longer one which can be cut off to fit), chalk for marking fabric, two brightly colored buttons each 1⅛″ diameter, one large brass snap fastener (#4 size or larger), darning needle, embroidery thread (optional, for decorative stitches)

1. If you are planning to create your own pillow designs, measure and mark two pieces of sketch paper the pillow size, 15″ x 26″. Allow a ½″ margin inside all edges for seams. Plan your front and back panel designs using simple, fairly large shapes which will be easy to cut out and to sew around.

If you prefer to make the designs shown at right, see the patterns on pages 82-83 and follow directions below.

In either case, begin by cutting two 15″ x 26″ pieces of background colored fabric or felt. If you are using your own

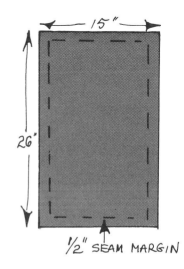

74

OTHER DESIGN IDEAS:

BUTTON

SNAP

POCKET MOUSE

TIE

ZIP

PILLOW FRONT

PILLOW BACK

USE NUMBERS OR LETTERS

designs, sew them onto background panels as in steps 9 and 15; then complete pillow by sewing front and back panels together as in step 16.

2. To make paper patterns from our designs, see pages 82-83. First read instructions written on each piece. Then measure, mark, and cut paper rectangles the size of the dotted outlines shown. Inside these outlines, draw freehand the shape desired. The details of each can vary as long as the basic form is close to the size shown. For example, the dotted line around the face outlines a rectangle 8½" x 15"; the solid line within this space shows the shape to draw (a). After making each pattern, pin it on the right side of the fabric (b) and cut around it. To help you identify the pieces, write the name of each piece on its pattern and leave the patterns pinned on until you are ready to sew.

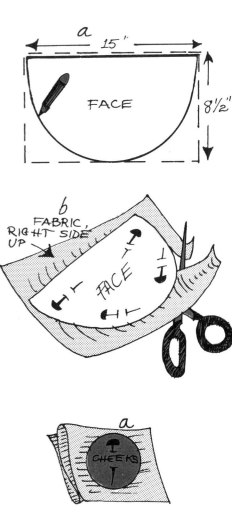

3. Cut as many pieces of each shape as indicated. If your fabric is not too thick, you can cut more than one piece at a time by pinning the pattern on top of several layers folded together (a).

To make hands, use the pattern in position shown to cut one shape from the fabric. Then make second hand by pinning pattern *wrong side up* on fabric before cutting it out (b). Cut shoes and arms the same way.

4. To make mouse, fold fabric in half and pin the pattern's base line along the fold before cutting. Do not cut through fold (c).

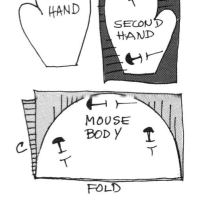

76

5. Fold the mouse body along the fold line with *right sides out.* Make the head at one end by overlapping and pinning the two ears between the body sides about 1½" above the point of the nose. Pin one eye on each side of the body as near the nose as possible, as shown (a). Pin, then sew the two body sides together along the dotted line; stop sewing about 2" from tail end to leave a hole for stuffing. The eyes and ears are fastened to the body at the same time by this one row of stitches. Remove pins. Push stuffing into opening until mouse is slightly rounded.

To make tail, cut three 24" lengths of medium-weight yarn. Knot them together at one end, set knot over a hook or nail, and braid to the end. Knot end. Stick one knotted end inside mouse's stuffed body. Pin, then sew remaining edges closed, fastening tail inside (b).

6. To make the zipper pocket, use a 5" zipper. If your zipper is too long, open it to the correct length as shown (a) and cut off the extra pieces.

Cut a line 4½" long down the center of pocket I, as shown on the pattern. Open the zipper and set it flat on the table, *right side up.* Place pocket I *right side up* on top of the zipper (b). Line up toothed edges of zipper with center cut in pocket; flat end of pocket is at top of zipper. Pin one side of the zipper to each edge of pocket's center cut. Fold under and pin down the top ends of the zipper (arrows) so they will not stick up above pocket. To sew zipper to pocket, place stitches about ⅛" over from zipper's teeth (dotted line). Sew a short straight row of stitches across bottom end of zipper. Sew a double row of stitches across the top folded-under ends of zipper.

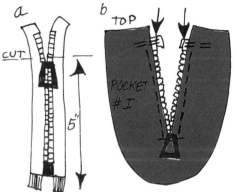

7. To decorate the front of the bow tie, cut, freehand, five 1″ to 2″ circles from a contrasting color fabric. Sew the circles to the front of one bow tie piece (a). Then pin front and back sides of the bow tie together, *right sides out.* Following dotted line, sew together all edges *except* on the underside of center curve (arrow, b). Stuff bow tie through this opening, then sew edges closed.

8. Cut buttonhole flap from the same color fabric as the face. Within this shape, cut two buttonholes, each 1½″ long, as shown. To do this, use scissors, poking a hole through fabric to begin the cut. Or set flap on scrap cardboard and cut slits by running a knife blade against the side of a ruler. **Be sure you have help or permission of an adult when using knife.** Sew over buttonhole edges with a close whipstitch, or sew around them with a small running stitch (page 13).

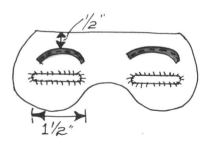

Pin, then sew down eyebrows above buttonholes and about ½″ below the top edge of the flap.

9. To complete front panel, set it flat on the table *right side up* and lay out the design on top of it. Arrange pieces according to your own plan or as described in steps 10 and 11. Be sure pieces fit together, then pin them in place. Set pins at right angles to the cut edges so you can sew over them. You can use one color thread for sewing on all the different colored pieces; the contrast in colors is part of the fun and the single color thread helps unify the design.

10. To attach pattern pieces, first pin down face, then hair on top of it as shown. Add buttonhole flap at forehead. Be sure to pin this piece only along its top edge so it can flap up and down. Later you will sew button eyes below this piece. Pin on nose, mouth, and cheek and chin spots. When pieces are properly arranged (a), sew them down, using running stitch (page 13). Stitch around outside edges of each piece *except* buttonhole flap, which is sewn only across top edge.

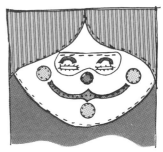

SEW PIECES DOWN WITH EITHER OVERCAST OR RUNNING STITCH.

To complete the eyes, poke chalk through the center of each buttonhole, marking the fabric beneath it. Then fold up buttonhole flap and pin it to hold it out of your way (b). Sew a button on each marked spot, making the eyes. Remove pins from flap and lower it; button eyes through buttonholes.

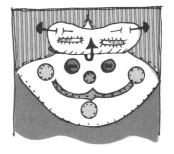

11. Make a chalk mark (X) about 1½″ below chin and pin (but don't sew) bow tie to this mark. Add arms, placing the widest end of each arm against the outside edge of background panel so it can be sewn into the seam. On the narrow ends of the arms, wrists overlap the hands, thumb side up. Sew the tulip and its stem just below the left hand. Sew knotted end of mouse's tail below the right hand. Add shoes, placing their soles ¾″ above the bottom edge of background panel; shoes do not get sewn into the seam.

12. To attach the bow tie, sew one half of a snap fastener to the spot below chin marked X. Sew the other half of the snap fastener to the center of the bow tie's back side. Fasten snap halves together to check position, then remove bow tie until pillow is completed (step 17).

SEW ON SNAP

13. Set pocket II below right hand on top of mouse's tail. Arrange tail so it rises straight up out of pocket top. Pin top edges of pocket only 4½" apart; this will make pocket puff out into a pouch to hold the mouse. Sew around sides of pocket, leaving tail free to move though it is anchored inside the pocket. Pin zipper pocket I on top of tulip so that it completely hides tulip when zipper is closed. Sew around sides of this pocket. The child who unzips it will be surprised to discover the hidden tulip.

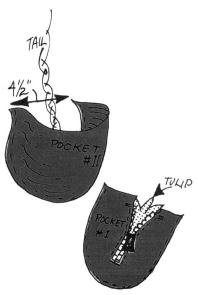

14. To make shoelaces, cut two 18″ lengths of bulky yarn. Thread darning needle with one length and stitch through front of shoe as follows: First stitch into hole #1. Leave about 8″ of yarn sticking out as shown and bring needle back out through hole #2 about ½″ away. Hold onto the first 8″ yarn end when pulling needle through. Then stitch down into hole #1 again (b). Bring needle back out through hole #2 and remove needle (c). You should have two loose ends of yarn, each 8″ long, fastened in the center. Tie a simple knot in each end of the yarn so it will not unravel. Repeat on second shoe. Tie laces into bows so they will not be caught in the seam.

15. To decorate the back side of the pillow with numbers or letters as shown on page 75, make patterns by drawing six rectangles, each 4½″ x 6″, on sketch paper. Inside each rectangle draw a bold fat number or letter as shown (a). Cut shapes out. Pin patterns to fabric and cut them out. You can decorate each number with small fabric shapes—one shape on number 1, two shapes on number 2, etc. (b). Small hearts, flowers, insects, stars, or birds can be sewn between the numbers or letters. Set the pillow's back panel *right side up* on table. Arrange the shapes as you like, leaving a ½″ border around the edges for the seam. Pin, then sew down the shapes.

16. To sew together front and back panels of pillow, first trim any long thread ends that may get in the way.

NOTE: TUCK MOUSE INTO HIS POCKET SO HE DOESN'T GET SEWN INTO THE SIDE SEAMS.

Place front and back halves together *wrong sides out.* Line up, pin, then sew seams ½″ inside three sides, as shown; leave one short end open for stuffing. Turn pillow right side out.

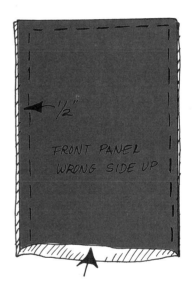

FRONT PANEL
WRONG SIDE UP

TURN PILLOW RIGHT SIDE OUT, THEN STUFF HERE

17. Stuff pillow until it is comfortably puffy. Then pin under the open edges and handsew them closed using whipstitch, page 13. Snap on bow tie.

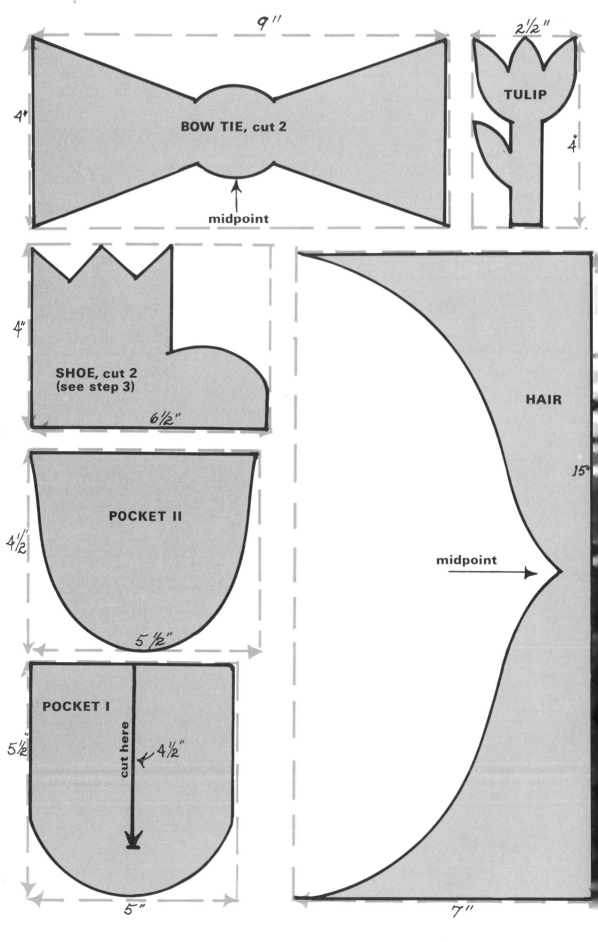

9"

BOW TIE, cut 2

4"

midpoint

2½"

TULIP

4"

4"

SHOE, cut 2
(see step 3)

6½"

HAIR

15"

midpoint

POCKET II

4½"

5½"

POCKET I

5½"

cut here

4½"

5"

7"

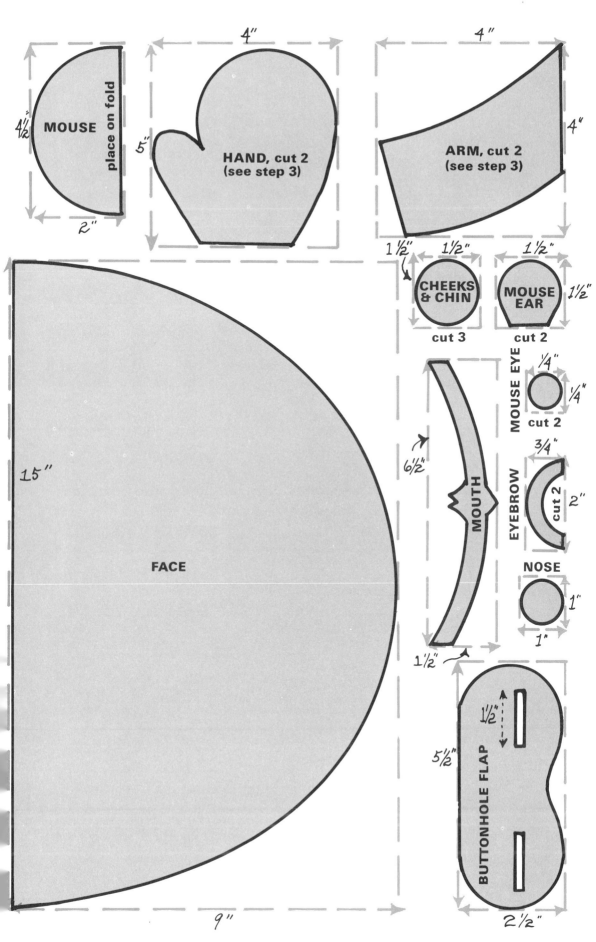

APPLIQUÉD GIFTS
Potholders, Quilt

These simple and quick-to-make potholders are decorative as well as practical gifts. And if you have lots of time and want to create something really special, you can make a great many potholders and sew them together into a fantastic quilt. This is a good project for a group to work on together.

Materials: Fabric (such as felt, sturdy cotton, or faded blue jean denim; for a quilt, be sure to use washable fabric), tape measure, scissors, pinking shears, padding (such as cotton batting or quilt lining—sold in department or fabric store), sketch paper and pencil, straight pins, needle and thread, sewing machine (optional), chalk (for marking fabric), café curtain ring (optional). *For quilt:* Embroidery thread and embroidery needle or colored yarn and darning needle, binding braid (optional)

POTHOLDERS

1. To make front panel of potholder, cut a 6½″ square of fabric. To make back panel, cut a 7½″ square of the same or contrasting color fabric. Also cut a 6″ square of padding about ¼″ to ½″ thick. Design is appliquéd (cut out of separate fabric pieces and sewn down) on front panel, then front is sewn to the backing and stuffed with padding. If you think your fabric will unravel easily, cut it with pinking shears; felt can be cut with regular scissors.

2. To plan design for front panel, trace around the outline of the 6½″ square on a piece of sketch paper. Draw a ½″-wide margin inside the edges as shown and plan design to fit in the central space.

Use bold, simple shapes that will be easy to cut out and sew down. Fine details can be added later with embroidery stitches if desired. Try cutting holes in some shapes to let the color of the front panel show through (as for the center of a flower).

3. Cut out pattern shapes. Pin them on fabric and cut around them. Remove pins and patterns from fabric. Pin pieces of design on front panel. Sew shapes down. To do this, stitch with sewing machine, or by hand using an overcast or running stitch (page 13); sew around all cut edges of each piece, including edges of any holes cut in shapes. Keep all knots on wrong side of panel.

4. Set back panel flat on table, *wrong side up.* Measure and mark points A and B, ½″ out from each corner. Draw chalk lines connecting the points as shown, then cut on lines, removing the tip of each corner.

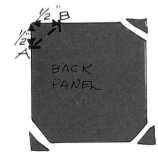

5. Center padding on the wrong side of back panel. Then cover padding with decorated front panel as shown (a). Padding is sandwiched between front and back panels, with ½″ border of back panel sticking out on each side. To complete potholder, fold the ½″ border over the edge of each side and pin it onto the front panel as shown (b).

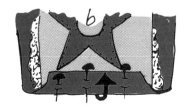

6. To sew potholder securely together, stitch along the edge of each folded border (dotted line), pushing your needle through all three layers.

Sew a café curtain ring in the center of one side as shown, or on one corner. You can make your own fabric hanging ring by cutting a fabric strip ¾″ x 5″. Fold strip lengthwise in thirds, then sew down the middle. Stitch ends together into a loop.

QUILT

1. To make a twin bed size quilt (roughly 39″ x 71½″), make 66 potholders as previously described. To make a larger quilt, add as many more 6½″ squares as are needed to reach the desired size.

2. Sew potholders together in eleven rows each containing six squares. Arrange the potholders face up on a bed or the floor. When ready to sew, place two squares side by side, face up, and stitch their edges together by hand, using an overcast stitch (page 13) or a decorative embroidery stitch. Sew with two-ply (or heavier) embroidery thread and an embroidery needle, or colored yarn and a darning needle. Add more squares alongside those sewn to complete each six-square row. Finally, sew all eleven rows together.

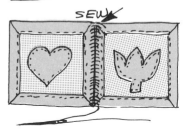

3. If you wish, you can sew overcast stitch around the outside edges of the entire quilt to give it a more finished look. Or cover the edges with a binding strip made of fabric—with edges turned under—or flat binding braid (found in fabric stores). Use 2″ or 3″ wide binding strips, each one cut the length of one side of the quilt. Fold and pin a strip in half over the edge of each side, as shown. Sew binding down, overlapping strips at corners and stitching through all quilt layers. Trim all loose threads and remove all pins.

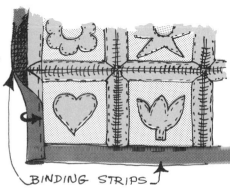

BINDING STRIPS

PATCHWORK GIFTS
Pillow, Apron, Bib Apron

Sew together nine squares of fabric, and you have a patchwork panel that can become a decorative pillow cover, a regular apron, or a bib-style apron. The aprons are scaled to fit two sizes: an adult and an average-size ten-year-old. This project is very easy to make and will appeal to nearly every person on your Christmas gift list.

Materials: Scraps of differently patterned fabrics (cotton or other washable fabric for an apron; use any fabric from cotton velvet to felt or satin for a pillow), tape measure, scissors, straight pins, needle and thread, sewing machine (optional), iron and ironing board, chalk for marking fabric. *For pillow:* Stuffing (clean rags, foam rubber, kapok, etc.). *For apron:* 2"-wide grosgrain ribbon. *For bib apron:* 20" x 9" piece of fabric for bib, ½" to ¾" wide grosgrain ribbon, safety pin

1. To make an 18" square patchwork panel for the front half of a pillow cover or the skirt of an adult-size apron, cut out nine 7" squares of fabric. Try to select fabrics of similar weight. To make a 15" square patchwork panel for a smaller pillow or an apron scaled to a ten-year-old, cut nine 6" squares. Directions are the same for both sizes.

2. Lay the squares out flat, in three rows of three squares; move the pieces around until you like the arrangement. In their final position, the squares in our example will be numbered as shown.

1	2	3
4	5	6
7	8	9

3. To sew the squares together, begin with the top row. Place squares #1 and #2 *right sides together* with square #1 on top. Pin, then sew a seam ¼" in from the left edge (dotted line, a). All seams should be roughly ¼" wide, and sewn either by hand with a running stitch (page 13) or on a sewing machine. Remove pins. Then fold back square #1 and place square #3 face down on #2 (b). Line up edges; pin, then sew #2 and #3 together along the right edge. Remove pins.

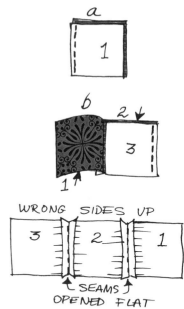

WRONG SIDES UP

SEAMS OPENED FLAT

4. Repeat step 3 to sew together squares #4, #5, and #6 in one strip and #7, #8, and #9 in another strip. Turn each sewn strip *wrong side up* and press a warm iron between the sides of the seams, opening them flat as shown. Cut off any long hanging threads.

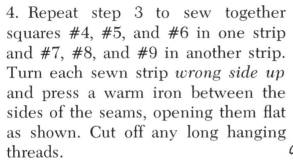

5. To sew the strips together, first arrange them *right side up* as they were in step 2. Flip the middle strip over, *wrong side up*, onto the top strip so that square #4 covers #1, #5 covers #2, and #6 covers #3. Pin, then sew a ¼"-wide seam along bottom edge of strips as shown (a). Remove pins.

Then fold down middle strip and cover it with bottom strip, placed *wrong side up* so squares #7, #8, and #9 cover #4, #5, and #6. Pin, then sew a ¼"-wide seam along bottom edge (b). Remove pins. Fold down bottom strip to see finished panel. Turn it *wrong side up* and iron all seams open flat as in step 4.

COMPLETED PANEL

PILLOW

1. Follow steps 1-5 above to make patchwork panel. Trim any uneven edges and hanging threads.

This panel is the front of the pillow. For the back, you can either make a second patchwork panel, or make the back from a solid piece of fabric.

To do this, place the patchwork panel on top of a piece of fabric. Pin the edges down and draw around panel with chalk. Remove patchwork, then cut out fabric, following drawn lines. Panels should be the same size.

2. With their *right sides together*, pin, then sew the front and back pieces together on three sides, making ½"-wide seams.

3. Turn pillow cover *right side out* and fill it with stuffing. Finally, turn under and hand-stitch the fourth side closed.

STUFF

APRON

1. Make patchwork panel following steps 1-5, pages 87-88. Place completed panel *wrong side up* on table with squares #1, #2, and #3 on top. On both sides and along bottom edge, make rolled hems (page 14) with their first fold ¼" wide and their second fold ½" wide. Pin, then sew hems. Remove pins.

2. The waistband should be as long as the wearer's waist measurement plus 30". A waistband 56" long would probably fit most adults, and one 52" long would probably fit most ten-year-olds. Cut 2"-wide grosgrain ribbon the right length. Cut the ends on a slant. Fold ribbon in half crosswise and put a pin at the fold to mark the midpoint.

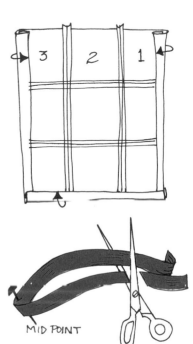

MID POINT

3. Fold patchwork square in half with its *wrong side out* and squares #1, #2, #3 at the top; place a pin at midpoint of top edge as shown.

4. Set waistband flat on table, *wrong side up;* set patchwork on top of it, lining up pins as shown. Keep both pieces in this position. Fold down about ½″ along top edge of patchwork and pin it to the waistband. About 1″ of waistband should stick up above hemmed edge. Sew hemmed top edge to waistband (dotted lines). Remove pins. Iron apron.

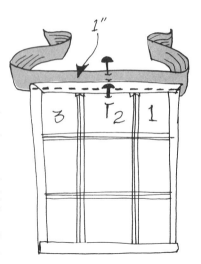

BIB APRON

1. Make a patchwork panel (pages 87-88, steps 1-5). Bib is made from a solid piece of fabric sewn to the top of the patchwork. This piece can be the same fabric as one of the patches or a completely different design.

   To make the bib for an adult-size apron, cut fabric 20″ x 9″ as shown (a). Long sides go at top and bottom. Along the top edge, measure and mark points A and B, 4″ in from the corners as shown. Distance between A and B is 12″. Draw one line from A to bottom left corner and another line from B to bottom right corner. Cut along these lines.

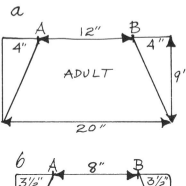

   To make ten-year-old-size bib, cut fabric 15″ x 7″ as shown (b). Points A and B are 3½″ in from corners, and distance A-B is 8″. Draw slanted lines and cut along them.

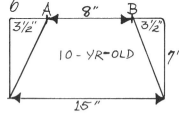

2. Place bib *wrong side up* and sew a rolled hem (page 14) in the top edge as shown. First fold of hem should be ¼″, second fold ½″.

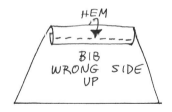

90

3. Sew rolled hems in both sides and bottom edge of patchwork panel, following Apron step 1 on page 89. Do not hem top edge.

4. Place patchwork panel *right side up* on table, unhemmed edge at the top, as shown. On top of this, place bib *wrong side up*, with its long edge lined up with top of patchwork. (If bib is wider than patchwork, center it before sewing, so equal-sized points extend past each side of panel. After sewing, cut off these points.) Pin, then sew pieces together along their top edges (dotted line). Place stitches about ½" in from edge.

5. Turn entire apron *wrong side up* and iron seam open flat as in step 4, page 88. Keep apron wrong side up. On each slanted side of bib, make a rolled hem (page 14), with both folds 1" wide. When you turn fabric under to make hem, corners of the patchwork panel will fold over along with the bib (arrows). Place stitches near fold of hem (dotted lines) so you leave open a narrow "pocket" to hold the apron ribbon.

6. Cut a piece of ½" to ¾" wide grosgrain ribbon, 8′ long for the adult-size apron or 6′ long for the ten-year-old size. Cut ribbon ends on a slant so they will not unravel. Fasten a safety pin to one end of ribbon and push it through the seam pockets on apron as shown (a). Remove pin. To wear completed apron (b), put ribbon loop over head and tie ends behind back.

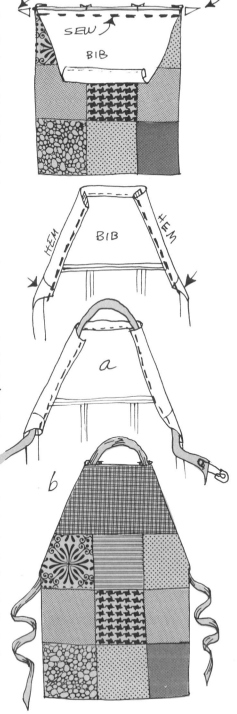

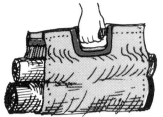

LOG CARRIER

This is a welcome gift for anyone who has to carry fireplace logs into the house.

Materials: Strong fabric (such as canvas, heavy-duty denim, duck, or upholstery fabric with a tight weave), scissors, tape measure, two wooden rods 26″ long and about 1″ in diameter (dowels or sawed broom handles), straight pins, needle and heavy-duty thread and thimble or sewing machine with heavy-duty thread, chalk for marking cloth, felt (for binding edges—either the same color as carrier fabric or a contrasting color)

1. Cut two pieces of strong fabric, each 32″ x 48″.

2. With *wrong sides together,* place one piece of fabric over the other in position shown. Line up and pin edges together. With chalk, mark two lines (X) about 6″ in from the long edges and two lines (Y) about 8″ in from the short edges, and sew along them, stitching by hand or on the machine.

Keeping fabric in this position, fold over and pin a rolled hem (page 14) on each *long* side of fabric. Each fold of hem should be 1″ wide. Sew hems, stitching through all layers of fabric.

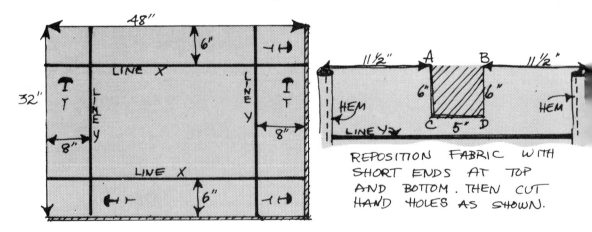

REPOSITION FABRIC WITH SHORT ENDS AT TOP AND BOTTOM. THEN CUT HAND HOLES AS SHOWN.

3. Cut out hand holes on both short ends of fabric. To do this, measure and mark points A and B, each 11½″ in from the corners of one short end as shown. The distance between A and B should be 5″. Measure and mark points C and D, 6″ down from A and B. The distance between C and D should be 5″. Draw rectangle A-B-C-D with chalk. Place pins around the outside of rectangle (striped area) to hold fabric layers together. Cut out rectangle. Repeat this step, cutting hole on other short end of fabric.

4. To bind the edges of the holes, cut two strips of felt, each 20″ long and 2″ wide. Fold one of these binding strips in half lengthwise over the cut edges of each hole, as shown. Make a little tuck in the felt as it goes around each corner. Pin, then sew the strips in place, with 1″ of felt showing on the front and 1″ on the back of the fabric. Remove pins.

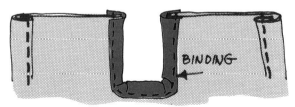

5. Place carrier in position shown (a), with inside surface facing up. The short panels on either side of the hand holes are folded over to make pockets for the wooden carrying rods. To do this, cut four strips of felt, each 1″ x 11½″. Fold 3″ of each panel over onto the inside of the carrier as shown (arrows). Pin one felt strip lengthwise along the unhemmed edge of each pocket. These felt strips hide the fabric edges and also connect with the felt binding around the holes, making a decorative finish. Sew around all four edges of each felt strip (dotted lines). Stitch through all fabric layers. Remove pins.

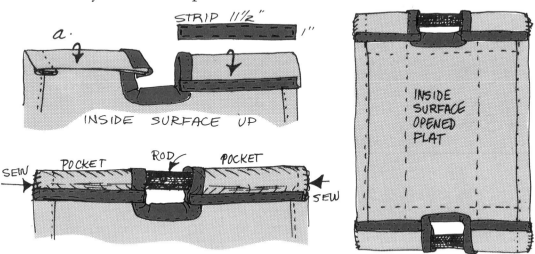

6. To complete the log carrier, on each end push a wooden rod into the pockets as shown. To keep the rods from falling out, stitch closed the outside edge of each pocket (arrows). To use, hold the carrier by both wooden handles and fill with logs.

GIFT WRAPPING IDEAS

1. Save containers all year long so you have a selection of packages for your handmade gifts. Use jars, discarded food containers, berry baskets, milk cartons, egg cartons, coffee cans, paper bags of all sizes, and cardboard tubes, for example.

2. For unusual and inexpensive gift wrapping paper, use shelf paper, plain tissue paper, or newspaper, hand printed or painted with your own designs. Or use colored funny papers, magazine illustrations, old sheet music, discarded drawings or paintings, scraps of fabric, or left-over pieces of wallpaper. To marbleize sheets of plain brown wrapping paper, float a few drops of enamel paint on water in a plastic-lined roasting pan. Set paper on surface of water, then lift it up; design will adhere to paper. Let paper dry before wrapping gift.

MARBLEIZED   SHEET MUSIC   WALLPAPER

3. Decorate packages to look like dolls, houses, animals, toys, trucks, etc. Trim them with cutout pieces of scrap packaging materials, magazine pictures, buttons (for making flowers or balloons), lifesavers or gummed notebook ring reinforcements (for truck wheels, eyes); you can also use lollipops, dry flowers or evergreen sprigs, star-shaped gummed seals, and pipe cleaners. Make collage designs by cutting out and gluing down pieces of colored paper, pictures from magazines, etc., or overlap pieces of colored tissue paper to make multicolored, semitransparent designs.

4. Make gift tags from cut-up bits of last year's Christmas or birthday cards. Or use old postcards, backed by plain paper. Cut tags from pieces of gift wrap to match the package. Or instead of tags, decorate packages with cutout name or initials of recipient.

5. Be imaginative when it comes to wrapping oddly shaped gifts. Some gifts, such as plants, should not be completely covered. Just wrap the base with paper or foil, or simply tie a gay ribbon around it and leave the rest exposed. A bottle or candlestick can be covered with a pressed-on sheet of foil. A flat gift like a pot-holder or gloves can be wrapped in an envelope or book mailing bag. Paper bags are great for holding gifts of all shapes. Use brightly colored bags, or paint your own decorations on plain brown bags. If your gift is lightweight, you can fold up the bag and cut out small triangles and circles to make a lacy snowflake-like pattern.

Surprise gifts are extra special. You can hide a small present in-side a cardboard tube and then wrap it to look like a firecracker or a flute. Or wrap a gift in a small box, then set it inside one—or several—larger wrapped boxes. Wrap jewelry in a broken-apart section of an egg carton, or in a paper cup decorated to look like a flowerpot, with a paper flower sticking out of it.

95

a

6. Many oddly shaped gifts can be formed into a basic cylinder shape. This will work well for a log carrier, candlestick, flowerpot (without plant), or wooden doll, for example.

a. Measure paper around object, allowing about 1″ overlap on sides and enough on top and bottom to cover ends. Mark paper at top and bottom edges of gift (dotted lines).

b. To make flat bottom and top surfaces, cut slits in top and bottom edges of paper as shown.

c. Roll and tape paper around gift, then overlap slit sections and tape them flat onto ends.

d. Cover ends with circles of matching or contrasting paper cut the right size by drawing around end of cylinder. Put a bow on one or both ends.

e. Another method is to roll gift in a piece of paper with very long ends. Tape paper in center to hold, then twist ends and fasten them with ribbons.

f. You can easily wrap a rounded form like a jar or bottle by setting it in the center of a piece of colored tissue or other flexible paper. Gather ends of paper together at top and tie with ribbon.

7. If you are mailing a gift, use a flat ribbon or a collage design to decorate package instead of a puffy bow which may crush. Follow Post Office regulations for size and method of wrapping boxes. Surround a fragile gift with crushed paper in its own box, wrap the box, then pack it in a heavy carton lined with twisted rolls of newspaper. Mark outside of carton FRAGILE, HANDLE WITH CARE. Tie boxes with twine or string.